EXACTING CLAM No. 17 — Summer 2025

CONTENTS

2	Jake Goldsmith	Remembering Gracián
4	Kurt Luchs	Maternal and Eternal Mysteries: The Interrogations of Louise Glück
7	Kurt Luchs	To My Chinese Daughters
8	Roy Lisker	Smokey
10	Marvin Cohen	On Hearing
12	P.J. Blumenthal	Two Poets from Dnepropetrovsk
16	John Patrick Higgins	Bang, Bang, Maxwell's Silver Hammer
20	Roberta Allen	Four Wise Women Who Were Not Always Wise
23	Shya Scanlon	An American Story
28	Dan Morey	Snigglefritz Flies
31	RW Spryszak	Time Tables
33	Kevin Davey	Moon scythes night's swirl of grain
36	M.J. Gilbert	Subverbs of Hell
38	John Oliver Hodges	Cornice Wild With Tongue
43	REYoung	Dreaming of Water in a Season of Drought
45	Joe Taylor	Timeless Love
47	W.J. Davies	The Man in the U-Bend
48	Ian Boulton	Futureproofing Against Nominative Determinism
51	Bradley David Waters	Bore Report Part Fore
52	Carl Landauer	She had been registered for Vassar at birth
53	Graham Clifford	Gift Tokens
54	Christopher Carter Sanderson	Elegiac, Amnesiac, Insomniac, Heart Attack
55	Jeffrey Hecker	Six Punctuals
56	Lucian Staiano-Daniels	Five Tanka
57	Ernest Hilbert	Nineteen Locks
58	Stefano De Vecchi	Love Poem (trans. Rose Facchini)
58	Irene Moccia	Contact Lenses (trans. Rose Facchini)
59	Alban Fischer	From "Human Arsenal"
62	Mike Silverton	Wunderhorn Honks
75	Julian Stannard	NOT IN TRANSLATION: The Litania /Litany by Giorgio Caproni. Untranslatable?
79	David Rose	Albertine Sarrazin's The Crib and Other Stories
82	Mike Silverton	Ron Padgett's Pink Dust
82	Charles Holdefer	David Galef's Where I Went Wrong
83	Jacek Blaszkiewicz	Mike Corrao's Surface Studies
85	Jesi Bender	Reviews in Brief: Josh Denslow, Hesse K., Emily Greenberg, Mark Doox
85	Laney Lenox	Em J Parsley's You, From Below
86	Michael Collins	Samira Negrouche's Solio
89	Christopher Boucher	Exact ng B rd

Front cover: *A Clam at the Bellagio* (2025) by Gina DeMartino
Interior art by Jake Goldsmith (p. 3) and Walter Smart

© 2025 Sagging Meniscus Press
All Rights Reserved

ISBN: 978-1-963846-43-0 (paperback)
978-1-963846-44-7 (ebook)

Contributing Editors: Jake Goldsmith, Tomoé Hill, Kurt Luchs, Melissa McCarthy, M.J. Nicholls, Mike Silverton, Thomas Walton
Contributing Metaclamician: Christopher Boucher

Senior Editors: Jeff Chon, Elizabeth Cooperman, Tyler C. Gore, Doug Nufer
Fiction Editor: Charles Holdefer
Poetry Editor: Aaron Anstett
Reviews Editor: Jesi Bender
Assistant Editor: Gina DeMartino
Executive Editor: Guillermo Stitch
Publisher: Jacob Smullyan
Exacting Clam is a quarterly publication from Sagging Meniscus.
exactingclam.com

Jake Goldsmith

Remembering Gracián

I have been re-reading Baltasar Gracián. I was gifted a copy of *The Art of Worldly Wisdom* some years ago and picking it up again felt easy, as it is slim and digestible while still greatly stimulating. Few do so well in so slim a book, but the quality of words means more than the quantity. Composed by the author as an oracular handbook, the reader feels free to open the text to any page to discover what awaits. As Gracián would agree, I read to work my mind—not my biceps with a heavy tome.

Gracián has always been acceptable to me, and an inspiration for others I'd also concur with. He distills the necessary contradictions of Montaigne into accessible affirmations rather than hiding his guidance in larger essays. Gracián's words are more difficult to take to heart, however, than philosophical or intellectual considerations I can easily store away and bring to hand when needed, as he often wonderfully expresses the best ways to behave, the best attitudes, ideas of graciousness and good judgement, the best ways to be prudent with our emotions and our impulses. He is the superego, suggesting how one should behave, although gratifying one's passions is easier. As such I often forget what Gracián says when it is most important in the heat of human interaction, and the wisdom is only recalled in hindsight. Memory is often unruly, or stupid.

Picking a favourite aphorism is difficult, but this one is particularly pertinent: "*Substance* is not enough, attention to *circumstance* is also required. A bad manner spoils everything—even reason and justice—a good one supplies everything, gilds, even sweetens truth, and adds a touch of beauty to old age itself. The *how* plays a large part in affairs, a good manner steals people's hearts. Fine behaviour is a joy in life, and a pleasant expression can help you out of a difficult situation in a remarkable way."

This seems eminently acceptable to me, even if I am personally poor at behaving well. It is a great example of an almost timeless cliché. It is good to be polite. It is good to know how to navigate a situation tactfully. Nonetheless some contemporary audiences will label this suggestion, especially in a volatile context, *tone-policing*; or insist it is an outdated form of 'respectability politics'. Sometimes malign groups will pick up and weaponise a good notion, which is often the excuse for abandoning good manners, given terrible people ask us to be polite, critique our methods, or demand we act with decorum. Yet we cannot allow them to rob us of good principles and good character. We may believe so much in the substance of a cause that any rude behaviour is tolerated. I object not to rudeness in itself so much as how ineffective it is and how self-righteous, and arrogant it is. One can be polite and arrogant too, but rude arrogance is the fad.

This results in moral activists (agreeable or not) who use such highly political language to become depoliticised. Real politics happens beyond and regardless of them while they performatively and expressively protest, rudely, or violently, or not—reduced to tedious slogans. They are not effective.

If impropriety works, then fine. But it often doesn't and many apparently cannot be convinced of this, as for them substance and personal grievances, however correct, because they are correct, seem to be enough. Tactics and tact are alien to them.

That these actions are resented is unsurprising. Without giving myself too much credit, I echoed[1] a similar sentiment: "It is not so much about being correct, I could reasonably say that my political opponents are terrible people or at least have terrible ideas, but this is complaining—not effective change. We can forgive ourselves for outbursts against the most horrible of people, especially when they have harmed us, or traumatised us, and we're not expecting people to speak and act politely. If impropriety works on occasion, it's welcomed. The real contention, here, is efficacy."

[1] In "A Brief Note on the Use of Aronian Liberalism," *Exacting Clam* No. 10, Autumn 2023. Reprinted in *In Hospital Environments* (Sagging Meniscus, May, 2024).

The nature of resentment is always poorly considered. Terrifying people who resent the appearance of superiority are unfortunately a great political force today. Moral-political activists, however technically or academically correct they are, would do well to consider this. Resentment of their hubris and bad form is what they generate more than good change. It is not so simple to denounce that truth. No reasonable person doubts the weight of injustice. That injustice is very real means one needs to be effective rather than only expressive. I care little for expressive politics that shouts and screams a lot, and may shout and scream all while speaking the truth, but leads nowhere.

I have not mentioned the useless, actively counter-productive free marketing for one's opponents in being so susceptible and easily distracted by trolling and bait. This is worse than involving oneself in petty scandals that debase anyone who speaks of them. So many resources are wasted in the theatre of superficially political content, while the physical, actionable designs of one's opponents press along unhindered and actively encouraged by salacious attention.

I dislike chastising fellow victims, yet the success of noble causes is dear, and too much action for good has somehow neglected better presentation, and believes it be hollow or needless, or a tool of our opponents. Many truly believe the substance of their injustice is enough. Again, no reasonable person doubts this substance, but it is never enough. Worse, the manner in which many activists present themselves is arrogant, hubristic, wasteful, contemptuous, cruel, dismissive, divisive, rude, vulgar, and sows deep resentment—all because substance is considered enough. When they face a deeply resentful backlash, when their divisiveness begets even worse illiberal behaviour, they cannot conceive of even a small part of this as being their own doing.

We are all, in various ways, responsible for how our peers behave—also when they behave badly. We can admit responsibility for this without being guilty. When my fellow citizens do something horrible, I am in some part responsible for it. Or rather, as citizens we are responsible for each other, but not guilty. The idea of being guilty for how others behave, as being one's own terrible fault, is such a pernicious feeling that even the subtle responsibility anyone has for how their actions affect others is too close an association and too much to bear.

If one is a victim of great injustice, it is comforting to find agreement in a comprehensive idea or movement that has brilliant answers and an exacting path to follow. Many such movements do speak the truth, and surely do note very real terror, but not always and not absolutely. If more honestly diagnosing the wrongs of the world means being more uncomfortable, and not providing definite answers, it is then painful to begrudge our dishonesty.

This will be dismissed. Extreme and revolutionary politics, rejecting such a quaint artifice as good manners and good form, are much more aesthetically and emotionally appealing. And therefore more easily intellectually convincing, even if dishonest. Once one is seduced by such an encompassing epistemological and ideological map of how everything works, whether decently coherent or closer to an inarticulate set of vague but powerful commitments, the world

The Art of

Worldly Wisdom

Baltasar Gracián

and events are answered. They just have to fall in line with one's agreeable ideas. If they don't, it is not your fault. Others maliciously interfered.

It is better to resist all such parables and grand schemes, whether from the left, centre, right, western or eastern, but that requires prudence and discernment, and living with uncomfortable tensions; with a sense of the unknown and unpredictability, confusing and contradictory instead of cogent and familiar. I am not stuck here, though. I am content to abandon good graces and be vulgar when it works, and I am happy to consider the tactics of brute force and immodesty instead of moderation and diligence. Gracián, as ever, has the ability to contradict me: "Do not take payment in politeness; for it is a kind of fraud." Or further, " . . . avail yourself here of the nimbleness of good form, for the same truth that wheedles one, cudgels another."

There is a danger in being excessively lucid, in not being impatient enough, though there is no shortage of impatient and vulgar sorts saying what needs to be said in different ways. Being *reasonable* is never so interesting.

*

Sometimes only brief words can produce superfluous thought. I'm sure Gracián was not considering the modern context of my intemperate peers, or my own folly.

I should not hold my views too firmly. "Every fool is fully convinced, and everyone fully persuaded is a fool." And more: in my above opinion, I am not the best at being courteous—surely, to some, I appear rude for suggesting so bluntly that many are vulgar or insulting.

The above, with all its pontificating, is speaking ill of people. I critique others harshly despite my own sensitivity and fear. "He who speaks ill will always hear worse." Something to worry about, but that worry will not always correct me. There is much to gain from Gracián, and a more concentrated effort in re-reading him may give me different insights each day.

Gracián's superego will have a hard time overcoming Goldsmith's id, which is sure to be forever ungracious. For all his talk of prudence and reserve I often do not follow, and I do not hold my tongue. Still, there is no one, however wise, who does not regret his youth or his embarrassments, or finds his memory disagreeable and wishes to demolish it for something far better. Yet I should not resent myself. One can only become wise, in the ponderous way we acquire wisdom, by recognising our risible or loathsome personalities that come before our better selves.

Wisdom appears easy but is often demanding to truly accept. Let us hope for some consolation.

Kurt Luchs

Maternal and Eternal Mysteries: The Interrogations of Louise Glück

The verse on greeting cards comforts us for half a second because it pretends to give answers and assurances: I love you, god loves us all, there can be peace on earth and goodwill toward men, etc., etc. Actual poetry, if it's any good, offers few assurances and even fewer answers. Like all the arts, it exists to give human utterance to thoughts, feelings and expressions that would never fit on something sold by Hallmark. Like the sciences, it poses the deepest possible questions about the nature of reality and our all-too-brief existence in it. Sometimes the questions are implied rather than stated, but they are always there, again, if the poem is worth reading at all. I'm thinking here, for example, of the implied question that concludes the brilliant Robert Frost sonnet "Design": "If design govern in a thing so small."

Poets are playful and mischievous creatures, the leprechauns of literature if you will, which is why they occasionally tweak us by pretending to ask trivial questions in order to surprise us with a sudden stab us to the heart. Could there be any question less consequential than the one asked by T. S. Eliot in "The Love Song of J. Alfred Prufrock," "Do I dare to eat a peach?" In the context of the poem, however, the question becomes devastating and heart-breaking. It continues to reverberate and even found a place in popular culture in the title of the Allman Brothers album *Eat a Peach* from 1972.

The Louise Glück poem we're looking at here, "Mother and Child," consists almost entirely of questions. It starts with implicit questions and ends with quite explicit ones. This movement provides most of the form in this succinct twenty-line piece of free verse. The rest comes from the poet's canny use of reiteration and what might be called variations on a theme. There are few overt poetics here, no rhyme, not even internal rhyme, and very little alliteration or assonance. It is stripped to the bone, the literary equivalent of Duchamp's artwork "The Bride Stripped Bare by Her Bachelors, Even" (aka "The Large Glass"), as laconic as a poem can be short of becoming pure silence. In other words, it is a typical Louise Glück poem, and all the better for it.

The title "Mother and Child" seems deliberately ironic, having been used by countless painters good and bad. She could have called it "Madonna and Child," but why drag Lourdes into it? The poor kid has enough to deal with. We know that Glück's poetry generally moves from the autobiographical to the universal. We also know that the most important relationships in her life were with her mother and her younger sister, territory covered in the final book published in her lifetime, her first and only fiction *Marigold and Rose* (2022).

"Mother and Child" is from her ninth book, *The Seven Ages* (2001). Many of the poems in this collection ponder her mortality and this one does too. More than the others, though, this poem seeks to peer back through time to a number of essential beginnings: the beginning of her life and consciousness, and by extension the beginning of all human life and consciousness. The twenty lines of the poem are broken into nine stanzas. The stanzas in the first half—which I take to be the first six—are all one or two lines long. Here are the first two:

> We're all dreamers; we don't know who we are.
>
> Some machine made us, machine of the world,
> thee constricting family.
> Then back to the world, polished by soft whips.

The first stanza implies that we can't know ourselves until we awaken from our dream state. The dream state is where we all begin and many of us never leave it, never achieve consciousness or self-awareness. There is such a thing as guided dreaming, where you learn how to direct your dreams and how to remain aware, within the dream, that you are dreaming. That's obviously not what Glück is talking about here.

"Some machine made us," she begins in the second stanza. By immediately refining this down to "machine of the world," she seems to be referring to what evolutionist Richard Dawkins calls "the blind watchmaker." Where is god or the possibility of god in all this? Napoleon asked French mathematician Pierre-Simon Laplace the same question, to which Laplace famously replied, "Sir, I have no need of that hypothesis."

She further refines the image down to "the constricting family," one of her favorite subjects. Every family is its own kind of machine, or its own system. As economist F. A. Hayek might have said in another context, each family is "the result of human action but not of human design." (he was talking about the self-organizing aspects of the market). Our parents pass on to us the haphazard genetic inheritance they received from their parents, along with whatever random sense or nonsense or absolute madness reigned in their families. And so we are shaped.

Now comes one of her best lines: "Then back to the world, polished by soft whips." What a haunting phrase! It isn't absolutely clear whether it's the family or the world that provides the soft whips, which gives it a rich ambiguity, but the structure of the stanza and the line implies the latter. It sounds as if in Glück's family, as in mine, the whips were seldom soft. Also, I'm guessing in her case the whips were metaphorical, not literal as they were for many of us.

The single line of stanza three provides a reiteration of and a variation on stanza one, except that instead of not knowing who we are, there is the broader statement "we don't remember." Don't remember what? Presumably anything.

Stanzas four through six consist of two lines each. They begin to move the poem forward after the provocative scene-setting of the opening. The "Machine of the world" is further refined to "Machine of the mother," and refers mysteriously to the "white city inside her." What is that? I have no idea. It's an evocative phrase but I don't know what it's evoking. Stanza five turns the clock back further to a time when there were no humans or animals of any kind, only "earth and water" with moss, leaves and grass. There is one final leap back backward in stanza six, where she speaks of " . . . cells in a great darkness. / And before that, the veiled world." Of course the world is veiled in the sense that the earliest fossil record is so scant and difficult to interpret after four billion years. However, I think this is also where the poem turns, where metaphysical mystery gets added to scientific mystery. The world is veiled and the meaning of it even more so.

The last half of the poem is comprised of stanzas seven through nine. Stanzas seven and eight have three lines each, more than any others so far, and the poem concludes with the almost fulsome four lines of stanza nine. One way of looking at this structure is that Glück paints a strange, disturbing picture in the first half, and spends the second half commenting on it and interrogating it with increasing urgency as her anguished questions accumulate.

Stanza seven starts with a bang (apologies to Ethan Siegel): "That is why you were born: to silence me." After all the metaphor and mystery of the previous stanzas, this straightforward, utterly assured declaration is a bit shocking. Some mystery remains, though. Is she talking about her own son, her only child Noah, to whom the book in which the poem appears is partly dedicated? Or is she taking her mother's voice and referring to herself? As best as I can figure, she means it both ways. The stanza continues: "Cells of my mother and father, it is your turn / to be pivotal, to be the masterpiece." Again, the same cells are in her and in her son. There is a great matrilineal chain of being, and not simply with the mitochondrial DNA, but with the mother who nurtures and constricts and polishes with soft whips.

After a brief reiteration of and a variation on stanzas one and three—"I improvised, I never remembered"—the poem races to a frantic ending:

> Now it is your turn to be driven;
> you're the one who demands to know:
>
> Why do I suffer? Why am I ignorant?
> Cells in a great darkness. Some machine made us;
> it is your turn to address it, to go back asking
> what am I for? What am I for?

That last question is as old as humanity and as current as the 2024 Oscar-winning song by Billie Eilish from the movie *Barbie*, "What Was I Made For?" Plaintively, piteously—but also, as she says, driven—she must repeat the question. The reiteration underscores the sorrowful fact that she got no answer the first time. If she had, she might also be able to answer the questions that begin the final stanza: "Why do I suffer? Why am I ignorant?" Wiser people than myself have long postulated that suffering is essential to understanding and embracing our purposes as humans on planet earth. Without it, how can we possibly have empathy? How can we comprehend and begin to correct our potential for harm as individuals and as a species? How, to return to one of this poem's central metaphors, can we ever hope to step out of the machine and achieve genuine consciousness?

As for being ignorant, yes, we are born that way. Many of us then spend the better part of our life's energy striving to remain that way, engaging in various forms of denial. We eat something called "food" that does not nourish. We take in something called "news" that, these days, seldom contains a single verified fact, only hate, outrage and contempt aimed at furthering a particular ideology or party. When we do engage with our emotions, we send and receive greeting cards, skimming the surface of our feelings, carefully avoiding the depths.

One reason I have always treasured the work of Louise Glück, particularly in poems like "Mother and Child," is that she "demands to know." She asks the hard questions. She kept on asking them right up to the end. And unlike our so-called leaders, she doesn't pretend to have the answers when she doesn't. As Covid should have taught us, ignorance is not the worst thing that can happen to us. It's curable, and both art and science are part of the cure. There is nothing worse than the pretense of knowledge, the delusion of competence. Both have killed or injured so many of us these past few years.

I love Glück because she acknowledges that ignorance is our starting point yet she refuses to let it be our end point. If you want cheap sentiment and superficial cuteness, go to Hallmark. If you seek truth and wisdom, go to the hard cold beauty of poems like this, which I believe compares favorably with the later work of Yeats. Go to Glück.

KURT LUCHS

To My Chinese Daughters

We didn't make you
your adoptive mother and I
but you made us

Your Chinese mothers made you
and either didn't love you enough
to keep you

fearful of the one child law
or loved you so much they had
to keep you alive

even if it meant hiding their pregnancies
at great personal risk and sacrifice
giving birth in secret (I prefer that version)

hidden in a city apartment
or a hut in the countryside
muffling their cries through the night

no doctors no nurses no morphine
then suddenly there were two cries
in the room

and there you were each of you
a fresh new living soul
and a problem to be solved

Having loved you all the way to birth
the limit of human endurance
in the China of that day

the question was where to drop you
where you would survive a few hours
until you were discovered

and sent to one of the country's
eight hundred orphanages
filled with millions of baby girls

plus a few boys with harelips
Nora your mother left you
at a hospital construction site in Xian City

home of the buried ceramic warriors
Jia they found you in a farmer's field
in Guangxi in the south

Each of you made it through months
in places where starvation and neglect
killed up to ninety percent of the children

and then you came to us
neither of us fully human
unfit to be married

let alone to each other
lost in every way a human can be lost
not knowing who we were

or why we were together
or what we were for
until they put you in our arms

Roy Lisker

Smokey

In *November of 1965, I and four others activists burned our draft cards in Union Square, earning us six month prison sentences. (Mine was served years later, in 1972, at Danbury and Allenwood penitentiaries.) Over that winter I occupied a bed in a dorm room managed by the Catholic Worker, the anarchist-pacifist movement founded by Dorothy Day in the 1930s. My roommates were all draft resisters and militant pacifists. One of them, Roger LaPorte, would later immolate himself on the steps of the federal courthouse in Foley Square in protest against the war.*

Between bouts of demonstrating, planning, and direct action I also helped out in the newspaper office of the Worker on the 3rd floor of the St. Joseph's House, then located at 175 Chrystie Street near the Bowery. I worked in a volunteer capacity. Besides myself the office held two regular staff persons: the painter Walter Kerrell, and Smokey. This account is about him.

Smokey was one of the legendary characters of the old Catholic Worker. He'd never been known under any other name. One might have described him as an alcoholic in semi-stable remission: from time to time he went on binges. By virtue of his many years of service to the *Worker* a dispensation had been granted whereby he, and he alone, was given the money to buy himself a six-pack of beer every Friday night. Only Dorothy Day herself had been at the Worker longer.

Smokey's life-long residence on the Bowery (New York City's Skid Row on the Lower East Side) went back four decades. With the enactment of Prohibition all the legitimate bars were closed and the derelicts were too poor to afford the speak-easies. This seems not to have affected the economic health of the Bowery, which was even more robust then than it is today. Apart from the historical fact that Prohibition never succeeded in reducing the amount of drinking, the Depression also increased the numbers of desperate people out of work.

"They sold us this shellac!" The standard confection, one to which Smokey gave his stamp of approval, was a mixture of Coca-Cola with shellac bought at a paint store. Sometimes denatured rubbing alcohol was used. One could get a bottle of shellac then for 15 cents.

"They made out like they didn't know what we was gonna' use it for! No sir! We just told'em we was paint'n th'floors! What th'hell—they didn't know the difference. So we was paint'n th'floors? They didn't care none."

When Smokey held court it was in a loud voice accompanied by arm-waving and dramatic gestures:

"We drank the stuff everywhere! In them days the 3rd Avenue Elevated was still standin'. We drunk it in the street; under the El; up on the platforms! They was the best places. If it was'a warm day, we'd be sitt'n or lie'n aroun' up there, from early in th' mornin' until it gets dark. In them days people got off at the Bowery at their own risk! It was okay, if you didn't mind stepp'n over bodies. Why, we was heaped up there higher'n a sinkful of dishes! If you was to ask me how I lived through it, 'till this day I can't tell you.

"But you take that *Sneaky Pete*[1] stuff they're drinkin' nowadays. That's wors'n anything! Nah . . . I would'n touch'a stuff! That *Sneaky Pete* drives a man crazy! And it ain't nothin' but cheap wine! That's all it is! You know that guy, crazy Mike, who's always comin'in here makin' trouble? He got that way drinkin' that *Sneaky Pete* stuff! I won't touch it. I wouldn't touch it if you give me all'uh money in the world! I wouldn't touch a drop of it! No sir!"

The pickled eyes in Smokey's much pleated and furrowed face glared at us over his thick horn-rimmed frames. He paused to take another long drag on the endlessly renewable cigarette that had earned him his nick-name, before continuing:

"Durin' th'Depression they turned some'a th'bars intuh soup kitchens. I used t'work at the one down'on'a corner, dishin' out soup. Later they sends me to Hart's Island. That's where they used to send us. They put us to work there, diggin' holes! Big ones, to drop corpses in. Yessir: even children! Kids! One day we carries 80 corpses up there, drops'em innuh holes, and covers'em over with dirt."

Walter Kerrell, who was in the office at the time, explained: "That's the Potter's Field. Dorothy wants to be buried there."

"Later they sends us back again to the Bowery, no better'n we was before. Them days you got all kind-sah people on the Bowery, young and old. Yep: lots of'em inn'er twenties! Lots of the folks you see on the Bowery got families. They comes down here to escape the disgrace. Here you drinks as much's you like, and nobody gives a damn. Nobody knows who you is! They comes down here't'escape the disgrace. They comes down here to drink themselves t'death!"

Smokey was in his 60s. The Bowery had prematurely aged him, the facial skin dry and taut on his skull like the membrane of a drum.

---

[1]   The cheapest Gallo wine

Though short and bony and clearly in poor health, he somehow appeared tough. Most of his teeth had fallen out; those remaining were charcoal black from accumulated nicotine. I never saw him without a lit cigarette in his mouth. Smokey had been laid up in the hospital shortly before I arrived. The first thing he said to Dorothy Day when she came to visit him was:

"Dorothy; has you got my coffin nails?"

She wouldn't have dreamed of coming without a carton. Casual visitors to the St. Joseph's House were well advised to bring a pack in case they ran into Smokey. The brand didn't seem to matter. And no one ever walked into the newspaper office without being cadged by him for 'coffin nails'. One reason for this was that he wasn't allowed much pocket money. What he earned through his office work was put aside in a fund for necessities. Even after 2 decades off the streets he was still liable to go on a drunk that ended only when he'd completely passed out. Walter Kerrell told me the following story:

Sometime in the early '50s Smokey slipped on the pavement in front of the St. Joseph's House and broke his leg. Despite whatever loyalty he may have felt for the organization that had rescued him from the streets, he sued the Worker. The judge ruled in his favor and he was awarded something like $10,000: a non-trivial sum even today. Although everyone knew it would go to drink, the CW had to pay up.

Over the next year Smokey did not step three times into the St. Joseph's House. Personnel and residents from the Worker would come across him lying against the buildings lining the Bowery, in the narrow alleyways and side streets, or under the tables of the local bars, out like a light. It took him a year to run through the award money. The CW picked up the pieces and eventually he was reinstated at his job in the newspaper office.

Smokey had even made the front page of the *New York Times*. Some years before he'd gotten a job washing dishes at an exclusive country club out on Long Island. While closing down the kitchen one weekend, someone accidentally locked him into the pantry. The following Monday morning his body was discovered, unconscious, in the liquor closet. Over this "lost weekend" he'd consumed the club's entire supply of Scotch! An ambulance took him to Bellevue Hospital. Walter couldn't recall if Smokey was rehired by the club.

To listen to him talk no one at the CW took more pride in their work than Smokey. Visitors to the newspaper office were given the impression that he was in charge of everything. The truth of the matter was that Walter Kerrell had been managing the office for many years. A few years later, however, Walter retired from the Worker and went out of his way to avoid it. The organization aroused fierce loyalty and fierce antagonism, sometimes in the same person. I think Smokey had died by that time.

Smokey's job consisted of entering new subscribers into a ledger and sending them the first issue. The CW newspaper is famous for its subscription policies: 1¢ an issue if you can afford it. Once you get onto the mailing list you are there for life, sometimes even beyond. I commonly saw newspapers returned that had been sent out to persons who'd died years before.

My job was to work the stencil-maker, a typewriter that manufactured the waxed-paper stencils that imprinted the addresses of subscribers to the CW newspaper onto slips of brown paper. These were wrapped around the copies folded and sent out by the team of recovering, (and sometimes not-so-recovering) alcoholics working on the second floor. It was also part of my job to remove stencils of deceased subscribers from the files.

One morning I arrived and found that Walter had placed a sign on the stencil-maker with Do Not Use written on it. The table and surrounding floor were buried in chunks of plaster both large and small, broken off as a mass from the ceiling not half an hour before. Had I been sitting there at the time I could have suffered a serious injury. Over the next month about forty pounds of plaster dropped from the ceiling into the room. Whenever it rained water poured down from three places. City health and fire inspectors who harass and sometimes close down anarchist operations are not always motivated by political malice. Fortunately the roof was fixed before the fire inspector made his yearly visit in April.

One Friday night a number of us were sitting with Smokey on the steps of his apartment on Kenmare Street, keeping him company as he drank his weekly six-pack. Apropos of nothing, he said:

"You know that work I do in the office? Any 6-year old could do that!"

He paused, staring bitterly at the pavement, his mask down, willing to confess to persons he knew and trusted what he would admit to no one else, the deep conviction that his life had been largely wasted:

"Any 6-year old could do that work."

Marvin Cohen

On Hearing

The Hear and Now

Being hard-of-hearing? I really don't know any different. To me, it's normal. Isn't *everybody* hard-of-hearing? No? Well, there must be something wrong with them, then. As for me, I may not hear, but I *am* here. That loudly proclaims my "sound" basis.

Stuttering Into a Defective Ear

I'm somewhat hard of hearing, so the words don't all come in right.

That balances *me* out: I *stutter* slightly, so the words don't all come out right.

Thank God we're not the same person, with the eccentric habit of talking to himself. For in *that* case, the self-stutterer would utter out broken words that would be further broken by the deaf ears' inability to take them in straight. What a completely incomplete circuit, concentrically ineffectual! No sense in being the same person, if *that*'s what happens.

No, it's better to be two people: one for speaking stutterless, the other for hearing without impediment. Then, something would be driven across. A mouth-to-ear communication, a safe delivery from port to port, with the cargo whole, intact, in a transference without incident. A sound message, sounded vocally, connected to its auditory goal with clarity of consummation. That's what two people are for, when one talks, and the other listens. An arrived home unit, healthy in transaction.

What an ideal! Are *two* people necessary?

Yes: unity in duality is more diversified than the single unity that oneness confers upon itself in solitary sameness.

Are then two heads better than one?

Yes. Clear speech, and sharp hearing: that's the key.

For such a healthy combination, I hope a worthwhile *idea* will be supplied.

Yes, what a lot of trouble cleared up for nothing, otherwise. For overcoming the twin handicaps of speech and ear, there should be an intellectual reward granted, a feast of mental depth in a verbal choice of light. Conversational nobility, is what we require.

You do truly aspire. May your high ideal have its commonplace success. A lofty thought well expressed and greatly received. How well for this to be so often, that the ideal rides disguised in a habit of ordinariness.

What did you say? I couldn't hear.

Sorry: my stammer made me indistinct. But *I'm* the deaf one, and *you* stutter.

Oh yes. Let's get our roles straight, to prepare our crooked transference better.

Yes, with our natural inabilities abetted by acquired impediments, let's serve as a double-barrelled vehicle for lame incomprehension, off to a wrong start and doomed to a futility of arrival.

Communication would fizzle out, wrenched to a short circuit.

It's the precise problem we bluntly ought to have. Symbolic, mutely, of a larger area expressing alienation of brother to man. This is an age of divorced souls, desperate solitude's reluctant falling back on its consoling miseries.

What?

I couldn't get it out properly. But I won't repeat. Let's rend the rendering of a snapped connected contact. *(Commanding:)* Back up. And so do I. *(They back up in opposite directions, till very far apart and still not stopping:)* Unsaid; unheard: a firmer guarantee. *(They've each disappeared in opposite wings, leaving the barren stage to puzzle out the dropping curtain.)*

Hear, Hear

The precious thing in life is to be bound together in ties of affinity with other people, to have your thoughts and feelings connected with their *thoughts* and feelings, on a good fair exchange rate. The instruments for this are talking, seeing, touching, hearing. I'm okay in the first three, but plagued in the hearing. It's so embarrassing to be the only one in a conversational group not attuned to what's going on: to be left out, excluded, alienated—even by the kind-hearted participants. The burden of embarrassment is harsh and hard: in being deficient in picking up others' utterance. Here I am, on the intended receiving end of people's precious links with me, they're offering me gifts of their ideas and feelings all wrapped up in packages of words—but the gifts aren't quite getting through to me. I'm on the receiving end but it's mainly a dead end, my receiving is too flawed, so people may give up telling me things, or humor me or baby me, patronizingly. Or ignore me. I'm a defective, not worth bothering with. They give up on me, write me off. I'm worthless.

Everybody wants to give out; and they're resentful and insulted if what they try to give out doesn't get well taken. Well, it's not well taken by me, but I can't help it, it's not my fault, it's a handicap, I'm hard of hearing, a little deaf, people must speak up, a little louder please, I'm hearing-impaired, hearing-disadvantaged, but not *stone* deaf; sometimes just enough gets through to tease and torment and torture me for the rest that gets blocked off. People offer package deals, and if you don't get the whole package they resent you and feel cheated, you're not validating their goods. You're not appreciating what's in them—what *is* them. You're undervaluing the people, by not hearing their very own personal words geared to you—*ear* marked for you. Yeah, *ear*marked.

This is my curse and it's getting worse, my loss seems to be progressive, my organ is slowly degenerating, I'm (he screams:) *being cut off! Cut off!*

It's like my cock would be cut off. I'm a king of social eunuch. I'm organically incomplete, not whole, unwholesome—a pariah.

Communication between people. I never underestimate its value, because I'm unfortunately never in a position to underestimate it. I can never afford to take it for granted.

So I compensate—I talk, talk, talk; I write, write, write. I give out words all the more, since alas I receive them all the less.

What are people saying? What words are they favoring me with?—If only I could thank them for these favors, by savoring these dear words that people are willing to throw my way. These words are bits of themselves. How can I refuse these bits of themselves?—I'm not heartless. I'm not *trying* to reject them. I appreciate the effort they make. If only I can avail myself of it. To complete the sacred precious circuit of these precious gifts of people's personal words getting well taken in understanding. I only get them in bits and bites—piecemeal. I can't devour the meals that people all too graciously, generously, cook up and serve. I'm undernourished socially—I'm starving. I have to take up the slack, the appalling gap, by talking and writing—to excess? I'm unbalanced. I give out more than I take in. It's my private budget deficit, trade deficit. Deficit? (Pointing to his ears:) *Deaf*-icit!

Marvin Cohen passed away on March 15, 2025 at the age of 93.

P.J. Blumenthal

Two Poets from Dnepropetrovsk

You have probably heard about Solomon Fishkin of Dnepropetrovsk who dropped his poetic works down a dumbwaiter shaft in a tenement building off Gorki Prospekt in November 1941 moments before a Waffen-SS commando bashed in his door and carted him off to his final solution. The consensus of his friends—and enemies—was that Fishkin probably would have avoided that fate—had he made the effort. Not only had he received ample warning about the likelihood of the raid, he also had had a variety of palatable opportunities to escape the city, including a personal invitation a year earlier from Abraham Cahan to come to New York and work for the *Jewish Daily Forward*. But true to character, this vainglorious "Yehuda Ha-Levi of the Ukraine", as he has been called, jockeyed his public image to the brutal end. "I hope this won't take long, gentlemen. You see, I have a very important meeting with my publisher this evening", he is reputed to have remarked to the steel-helmeted soldiers as he raised and heaved the door to his apartment, half off its hinges, back into place, even making a clownish attempt to bolt the lock with a heavy skeleton key—at least that is how his neighbor, Vera Prokovna, described the scene when interviewed shortly after the War.

You may recall his poem:

> Death cannot break down my door
> or wrap his shroud around my daily habits.
> Not me, my friend.
> I've ordered a predictable end.
> It's been waiting for me
> unseen, like all things future.
> Think of it as a lover's sweet kiss
> and a shared glass of wine.
> That is all I shall reveal:
> a few hints about an intimate reunion,
> expressed in simple Yiddish words.

Most admirers doubt he received his lover's sweet kiss or shared that glass of wine (Crimean champagne would have been more to his taste) with anyone, no matter how broadly one interprets the cosmopolitan coquetry of this poem, "My End" ("*meyn sof*" in the original Yiddish), a piece which tends to confirm that Fishkin's prophetic skills seriously lagged behind his poetic insight. Still, the fact that the bulk of this urbane poet's work—much of it unpublished in his lifetime—did manage to survive remains one of the minor miracles in the history of literature, comparable to the discovery of the vanished works of Catullus under a cask of wine in Verona around 1300, or finding Bacchylides' elegies on a papyrus roll wedged between a mummy's feet in Egypt in 1896.

It is truly an astonishing story which till now has only been partially revealed by the only person who could possibly know it, my neighbor—and I'm proud to say friend—Shaya Rachmanov. He has given me permission to tell it in its entirety . . .

In those dark days, Shaya was a dental technician and lived one flight up from Fishkin in that building off Gorki Prospekt, his apartment on the opposite side of the landing. Fishkin was barely aware of Shaya's existence, acknowledging him usually (if at all) with a perfunctory nod when they chanced to run into each other on the staircase. What he saw was a man, more or less his own age, but lacking in charisma or good looks. Probably if he had known Rachmanov was a dental technician, he might have been more inclined to exchange a few friendly sentences or proffer bits of flattery in the hope of currying some professional favor should he ever need dental work, dental appointments being notoriously difficult to get in those days.

Somehow Shaya was Fishkin's *antipode*. Whereas Solomon delighted in crowds and radiated a charm that made most everyone who had any dealings with him—in particular women and homosexuals—swoon, Shaya had a sullen character that might easily have been misinterpreted as misanthropy. For the most part, he remained invisible to his surroundings.

Of course, like many introverts, Shaya too probably would have enjoyed letting his hair down sometimes or being quick-witted and popular with the girls the way his downstairs neighbor was. He just didn't know how to go about it. On the whole though, he was content with his bare-bones asceticism and comfortable nurturing a quietly pessimistic worldview *à la* Schopenhauer. My guess is: had Solomon Fishkin gotten to know Shaya, he would have probably—like all extroverts—been attracted—or envied—the latter's outer quietude and the inscrutable depths of what appeared to be a melancholic soul, imagining the other as the calm eye at the center of the storm of existence. In other words, an utter contrast to himself. Most likely, Fishkin wouldn't have been able to cope with that sort of inner solitude for more than four hours running. He was as addicted to his audience of solicitous, pampering admirers as they were to him—even if deep down any true mutual affection was questionable. Moreover, it would have been impossible for him to forgo the attention he received from the coterie of spoiled and well-heeled industrialists' daughters who constantly attended him.

Making the acquaintance of Rachmanov might have interested Fishkin for another reason as well: Shaya, like his popular downstairs neighbor, was just like himself a poet, an industrious wordsmith, whose lyrical and erudite manuscripts were etched out in the privacy of his sparsely furnished tenement apartment, works of great power, unread, unpraised, unknown. A fact that would have pleased Fishkin, for he always showed great respect for other literary craftsmen.

It should be added here that the two poets were neighbors not merely by chance. Shaya Rachmanov had taken the initiative, being seriously interested in finding a suitable means of crossing paths with Fishkin without appearing to be pursuing him in some unctuous way. Managing the move into Fishkin's building, especially when you consider the housing shortage that prevailed in the city in those days, demanded unerring willpower. But Shaya, a pragmatic person, solved the problem easily by organizing an urgently needed bridge for a gap-toothed commissar at the Bureau of Habitations.

Like many introverts, Shaya was not afflicted by a blanket shyness. In situations that did not depend on "social skills", particularly when his survival was at stake, he was always a skillful player, ever ready to take all necessary risks—which explains, I should add, how he escaped his antipode's horrible fate.

You see, on the day Solomon Fishkin was arrested, that same commando also had orders to ascend one more flight in order to fetch him as well. Had they achieved that goal, I suppose Shaya would have finally had the opportunity to meet his neighbor—and perhaps they might have discussed poetry, at least briefly.

But Providence had other plans for Shaya Rachmanov. For at the very moment the *Einsatzkommando* was bashing in his downstairs neighbor's door, Shaya chanced to open his own door, ready to leave for work. Hearing the ruckus below, he immediately understood the urgency of the situation, which is to say that they were coming for him next. With only seconds to plan his escape, he dashed into his apartment and snatched what he most valued: his manuscript. He locked the door behind him and hurried across the hall to his neighbor, Madame Vizhenskaya, an officer's widow in her early nineties. Because of her hearing impairment, he bellowed his predicament into her good (relatively speaking) ear—speaking Russian so the Germans wouldn't understand should they take note of the talking upstairs. He had no doubt she would be willing to help him. Not only had he fixed her up with dentures—a practical profession like his is truly a godsend in hard times—he'd also regularly fetch wood from the basement for her stove and do some marketing for her. He entered her apartment and with cool-headed alacrity dropped his manuscript down the dumbwaiter shaft in her apartment only minutes after his famous colleague had done the same. Then, from behind his neighbor's door, he waited and listened. It was just as he had imagined: they were already hammering at his door. He heard a crashing and the snapping of wood, then the muffled sound of the harried Germans ransacking his apartment. He could not make out everything they were saying although he understood their language fairly well. When he heard them shuffling towards Madame Vizhenskaya's door, he reacted immediately. Not wasting a moment, he leapt into the dumbwaiter shaft and shimmied into the pitch blackness down the pulley rope, waiting silently below until he was certain the stymied storm-troopers had left the building obviously frustrated that they had accomplished only half their mission.

Groping in the dark, he felt around for his manuscript, tucked it into his pants and shimmied up the rope to Madame Vizhenskaya's apartment. He bade his faithful neighbor a triste farewell, packed a small suitcase and settled for the only option available to him: to head for the countryside and link up with the partisans.

It was only after he had joined ranks with a group of Jews and antifascist Ukrainians in a forest outside of Pavlograd that he realized his error: the manuscript he had smuggled out of Dnepropetrovsk was not his own, although outwardly it resembled his, which is to say, it was the same standard school notebook sold at every stationery shop in town. His heart sank and his stomach juices turned bitter. That was his first reaction, followed by flurries of panic, desperation, mourning, confusion and disbelief. Not necessarily in that order. He closed the notebook a couple of times and opened it again, each time almost willing to imagine that his eyes had been playing tricks on him as a result of the enormous strain of the past days. But no. As he leafed through the pages, it became indelibly clear to him: he had not saved his own manuscript but a volume of Solomon Fishkin's unpublished works.

Once the initial shock, a state difficult to describe in words, had loosened its grip—and that took a while—he began leafing through that notebook and reading the pages, poem for poem, marveling at the high quality of the work. Naturally, the more brilliant the piece, the more the sharp edge of envy and sorrow pierced his heart. Still, he knew he was in possession of something valuable, noble, something he felt obliged to protect like he might a helpless child or a rare jewel until the madness around him abated and he could return this cuckoo's egg to its rightful nest. And yet, those

pages, as precious as they were, never ceased to feel alien in his hands. Moreover, they served to remind him how much he pined for his own lost notebook, filled with so many words he had struggled so hard to find, to formulate, to fix in sweat and ink. Had circumstances been different, Shaya Rachmanov might have seriously considered returning to the dumbwaiter shaft in the tenement off Gorki Prospekt in Dnepropetrovsk to retrieve his own work. A wishful fantasy. A war was raging, and he and his comrades were slogging northeastward, daily drifting ever farther from his city on the Dnepr. Moreover, the enemy was sweeping across the countryside, and the continental winter was weighing in mercilessly. What could he do but tramp with his comrades through the snow, Fishkin's manuscript packed under his coat and fastened to his belly by a thick cord like a nursing infant, a captured German Karabiner 98k slung over his shoulder?

That was 1941. The War dragged on till one forgot it might ever end. Rachmanov veering ever farther from his city, first northward to Charkov and Kursk, then westward towards Smolensk and Minsk and southward to Bialystok and Bucharest. In the fall of 1944, he was entrenched at the west bank of the Vistula outside Warsaw along with the Red Army, poised for the decisive attack against the enemy. Finally, in April 1945, he rumbled into Berlin at the controls of a clunky Russian tank, rolling over the rubble of a city which lay in ruins like his own literary dreams. It should be mentioned that Rachmanov was not a poet whose subject matter had ever evoked any war between nations. He portrayed the struggles that raged within souls, a battlefield he had been seriously neglecting since fleeing Dnepropetrovsk. For four long years he did not hold a writing instrument in his hand. Instead, he had become eminently skilled in weaponry and had learned to kill with cannons, rifles, knives and even his bare hands. When the somber, battle-hardened dental technician from the Ukraine rode into Berlin, Solomon Fishkin's manuscript was still safely fastened to his belly, continually a cause of joy and sorrow. And yet, all those years, he had never given up hope of returning to his building off Gorki Prospekt to retrieve his own lost works from the dumbwaiter shaft. You might say it became his *raison d'être* to imagine a reunion with those abandoned poems whose content he could barely recall except to know that they incorporated the distilled expression of his soul through language. Years of yearning had transformed them into the fabric of an identity that had been frayed and torn by the exigencies of war. He couldn't even be sure they existed anymore, or whether the house where they had been hidden was still standing. What's more, or better said, what's worse, the world in which they had been conceived—the inner and the outer one—now seemed as distant and irretrievable to him as some ancient, buried civilization. And then there was that other question: would his poems still mean anything to him?

Now, wandering through the ruins of Berlin and knowing the War was in its final throes, he dared to imagine that soon it would be possible for him to return to that place of his dream cravings. But what if he discovered that during that terrible winter of 1943, when fuel had been most scarce, his wispy old neighbor, Madame Vizhenskaya, had fished his manuscript out of the dumbwaiter shaft and burned it. Could he hold it against her? "Gospodin Rachmanov", she would say to him, "I am very sorry to have to report this to you, but I used your lovely words to heat my kitchen. As you know, I do not understand your Jewish language, but I wish to tell you that your words were warm. They glowed and radiated heat for hours during the darkest days of the struggle to save the motherland". Or what if rats had eaten his words for lack of alternatives, or if the rain had leaked through the roof and liquidated his pages? What if someone had discovered the manuscript and tossed it into a rubbish bin or published it under his own name? What if I die now, and my work is still nestled in its hiding place like a seed waiting for its season to come? Maybe one day someone will discover it, but will they be able to trace the authorship back to me? Maybe a critical edition

will appear, accompanied by scholarly footnotes and various hypotheses about the references. If the manuscript is anonymous, as I expect it will be, they'll attribute it to the "Poet of Dnepropetrovsk" or to the "Dumb-waiter Poet". Or maybe to Solomon Fishkin!

Shaya Rachmanov did not make the journey to the Ukraine when the War ended. He continued on to Munich and Stuttgart and eventually emigrated to New York. There, thanks to him, the works of Solomon Fishkin he had salvaged from obscurity were published in Yiddish accompanied by an excellent English translation along with Fishkin's early works. In the introduction, the publisher thanked the dental technician profusely and briefly described the daring odyssey that had saved the precious cache of poems. Granted, he only knew part of the story. As for Shaya, he too contributed something to the book: a few lines of verse he had once scribbled down in a Manhattan hotel room, the first and perhaps last poem he had written since the War began. It served as a kind of motto to Fishkin's work:

> Some say the word came first,
>   others the soul.
>   God makes clay from both
> and potters turn them
>   into pots and shards.

Shaya Rachmanov never returned to Dnepropetrovsk. He stayed in America, married, had three sons, the oldest named Solomon, and became a successful dentist in a mid-sized New Jersey town. Meeting him today, it is hard to imagine him as a partisan. Nor would most people suspect the poet in him. You see a quiet, aging man in an American suburb who speaks English with an accent. His downstairs neighbor, Vera Prokovna, confirmed in a letter to him written shortly after the War that the house off Gorki Prospekt had survived unscathed. Madame Vizhenskaya had died in the winter of 1943. According to a recent query I made, the house is still standing. Sometimes I wonder whether his manuscript may be there in the basement, waiting to be discovered, unless of course someone has already found it.

John Patrick Higgins

Bang, Bang, Maxwell's Silver Hammer

He closed the door, leaning against it, grateful for the support. It kept the teeming world away. After a few seconds and with effort, he pushed into the house, slipping the Oi Polloi parka from his shoulders and hanging it over the edge of the banister. He went into the kitchen to warm the pot for a loose-leaf Earl grey with blue flowers. It was his personal blend, made for him exclusively by Steven Smith.

Perched on a stool in his cool, glass kitchen, he stared up at the bruising sky. The clouds mirrored the vortical motion in his cup, dense and sudden, like blood dropped into water. He shivered and held the exquisite China cup in both hands before catching himself. That wasn't who he was anymore.

The change had come from a blow to the head. In some cases, an early frontal lobe trauma can lead to an inability to control mood swings and a lack of empathy. A high proportion of serial killers have some evidence of brain damage, but for Liam it had been quite different.

It was an ordinary school day, and he'd had an ordinary difference of opinion with Max. Liam would often initiate differences of opinion, even when no obvious difference of opinion was forthcoming. He lived for friction, for the chance to off-load the anger that churned inside him. He didn't know where that anger came from—he could guess—but its provenance was of little interest. His rage was emetic, and he wanted it out of his body as quickly and violently as possible. He was always fighting, always acting up, always talking back, and he was always right, especially when he wasn't. But this time he'd made a mistake. He'd picked a fight with a bigger kid. Max had a head trauma of his own and needed to pass on the blessing. Liam had picked a fight with a boy with a hammer in his hand.

He finished his tea, went upstairs, and took a long, languorous bath in his cast iron double-slipper clawfoot tub. He shaved methodically without a mirror, guiding his bocote wood-handled open razor carefully over his chin, having lathered himself with extract of limes hard shaving soap, generously blotted with a badger-hair brush. While soaking in the tub, he glanced at an immaculate 1887 copy of Mallarme's *Poésies* in the original. It was a first edition, so he was careful not to get the cover damp. Liam didn't speak French, but he loved to read the words out loud like an incantation. They clattered off the black tiled walls, the gold inlayed grouting softening the impact to a degree. The floor tiles were Connemara marble and reminded him of green carbolic soap, one of the few happy memories of his childhood.

He dried himself with a towel so thick and soft he could barely bend it around his body. The slightest application to the skin drew water into its filaments, so Liam arrived at his dressing room fluffy and dry. He sprayed and stepped into a cloud of Penhaligon's *The Uncompromising Sohan*, and closed his eyes to better savour the lingering scent of rose and oud.

At his dressing table, he stared into the ornate antique triptych mirror, noting the hawk-like nose, the petulant lips, the pleasingly firm jawline. He hated his eyes: goatish and heavy-lidded, they were the eyes of a high-ranking Nazi officer: sleepy, supercilious and cold, both bored and arrogant. He hated his eyebrows even more. They were profuse and haywire. Lately they were getting worse, jutting out like antlers, a territorial challenge to passing impala. No wonder he hid behind his front door. He had the nose and mouth of a poet and the eyes and eyebrows of a troglodyte. Those eyes had seen charcoal smeared on cave walls, had witnessed reeking mastodons thrashing in pits of spikes. They had met those of Cro-Magnon men and realised the jig was up. If he had normal eyes and eyebrows, he would have looked like Chris Evans, the *Captain America* actor. Not Chris Evans, the irritating ex-husband of Billie Piper.

During his regular career lulls, when he could slip away from the cameras and the press, Liam was free to pluck his eyebrows, which he did with 17th Century porcelain-backed tweezers he'd bought at auction. He spent the days afterwards staring into a hand mirror that had once belonged to Grace Kelly, admiring the tightness, the control, the efficient and elegant framing of his face. Even his eyes looked better in this context: brighter, less like those of an ungulate. He fought back an impulse to pluck them again, but he had a photo shoot supporting the new album booked for next week. The best he could do would be trim back the more wayward antennae, some of which forked out an inch if left untamed.

*He'd woken up with his head turbaned and his senses displaced. Nothing was quite right. Everything felt like it had been bustled out of the way to make room for something new and important that was coming, and Liam was certain **he** was the coming thing, the thing the world was waiting for. The universe was pushing through him like light through a prism. He prodded at the tight ball of linen binding his head. This was the focal point: something like the ghost of pain echoed out of him in soft buttery ripples. He was in a hospital, and he couldn't remember why he was in a hospital.*

There was a little jaundiced man in the bed opposite with cavernous hollows where his cheeks should have been. He was listening to a cricket match on the radio, an earpiece pressed to the side of his head. His hair was neatly parted and fell in thick oily waves. It seemed unnaturally lustrous for his cheese-paring face. The match concluded to his obvious dissatisfaction, and his papery fist bounced off the Telegraph resting in his lap. He tugged at the earpiece and, in his passion, disengaged it entirely from the radio. The ward filled with the sound of music. And what music! A joyful noise unto the creator. Liam goggled. He felt as though he'd stepped into a new world, clothed in white raiment. The ward seemed busy with new colour and detail, the sick and the dying now invested with poetry and legend. They were dignified and benevolent, where previously they had been screaming and smelling of urine. The old man's narrow face darkened, as his fingers moved toward the radio's dial. Liam leapt from the bed and snatched the radio from the old man's hands, pressing it hard against his bandaged head. He felt the bass pulsate through him, the drums hard as punctuation through some heavenly decree. But it was the singing, the choral, exultant singing that brought tears to his eyes.

"Just like a prayer I'll take you there".

It was an invitation to a celestial kingdom and Liam was rocking up to the pearly gates. He stood there shaking, eyes shut, leaking tears, while the little yellow man called for a nurse.

After this revelation Liam was insatiable. He devoured music and music opened him up to everything. It cleansed the doors of his perception and, where previously his chief interests had been footie and fighting, he now embraced the world:

Wings of Desire, Betty Blue, Beethoven's 7th, Subway, Meat is Murder, The Outsider, Nausea, If On A Winter's Night A Traveller, La Belle et la Bete, The Bicycle Thieves, M. Hulot's Holiday, Die Rosenkavelier, Tago Mago, The Man Who Mistook His Wife For A Hat, Performance, Drowning By Numbers, As I Lay Dying, Notebooks of Malte Laurids Brigge, Death In Venice, Night of the Hunter, The Poison Boyfriend, The Big Blue, In Cold Blood, Being There, Erik Satie, Berlioz, Le Quatre Cents Coups, La La La Human Steps, This Mortal Coil, Lonely is an Eyesore, Benjamin Péret, Paris Peasant, Pink Moon, Shelleyan Orphan, Mitsouko, Vetiver, Letter from an Unknown Woman, In a Lonely Place, The Unbelievable Truth, In Gardens where we feel secure . . .

Liam decided to start a band. He knew he had a long way to go before he could realise a *Symphonie Fantastique* like his hero, Berlioz, but fire had been kindled in his soul and he had to act, despite the paucity of materials available to him. He had no money and no access to an orchestra, but he did have a flaming desire to create and was realistic about his compositional skills. He would need to nurture the flower of his gift over time.

To this end, he recruited two school friends: Paul, whom he nicknamed "Bonnard" after one of his favourite painters, and Paul, whom he didn't give a nickname. The band was called *La Reine*, after the Dumas novel, which the other two were fine with. The initial compositions were disappointingly flat, lifeless doodles, over which Liam intoned his Valéry-inspired verse to little effect. It was dispiriting: the insipid strumming, the leaden bass, his voice unformed; the cadence of the lines was wrong, falling between missing beats. The first song he'd ever heard, bandaged in that stifling hospital ward, had shown more wit and imagination than the nonsense he was creating, and his sensibility had grown far beyond that pseudo-gospel dirge by now. The gulf between the music he could make and the music in his head seemed unbridgeable.

Liam sat alone in the corner of the rehearsal space, the ink on the cramped pages of his lyric book blotted with tears. Paul and Paul jammed noisily. Paul had bought a delay pedal and was anxious to try it out.

"Liam! Listen! I'm the fucking Edge."

He played a simple guitar figure that clanged about the dingy space.

"That's fucking mint, that," said Paul.

"Yes, Paul," said Liam, solemnly, "most diverting."

"I hear you fuckers are looking for a drummer."

Silhouetted in the doorframe like an Athena poster, was a young man with wide shoulders and a wider grin.

"Beesley's the name," he said, "and skins are the game. Both kinds." He gave a wink and Paul laughed.

"Welcome, friend," said Liam. "In truth we are in dire need of the spine of syncopation. For we are sprawling and flat, like the suckered mollusc dredged from the keep-net. We crave your support, sir."

"Yeah, I know. I heard you outside. Like the fucking Alarm or something."

"Well, not that bad," said Paul.

"Sorry," said Beesley, "well look no further: the prince of percussion is about to . . . hang about, mate. Do I know you?"

Liam started. There *was* something oddly recognisable about this Beesley, his gait, the way he carried himself. It struck Liam, suddenly, with a familiar violence.

"You were that geezer I knocked on his arse," said the drummer.

"Yes," said Liam, "and I owe you a debt of gratitude, sir. You have given me . . ."

"This bloke, your mate . . ." the drummer rounded on the Pauls, "started on me, and I knocked him spark out in front of everyone."

Paul and Paul shifted uncomfortably.

"Yes, but the point is . . ." said Liam.

"Spark out," said Beesley, "with a vibraphone mallet—yeah, I also play vibraphone. Have you seen a vibraphone mallet? It's like a toffee apple made of leather. Its padded—you couldn't knock out a dandelion with it, but this fucker was in the hospital." He laughed heroically, fists on hips.

Liam no longer felt like telling the newcomer about the vast improvement he'd made to his life, however accidentally. There didn't seem much point. The boy was more interested in gloating and importuning the others who were, predictably, already laughing.

There was a loud resonating clang and Beesley, still grinning, sank to the floor. Behind him, guitar still humming in his hand, stood Liam's brother Noel. He jerked his chin out in recognition, before looking down at the slumped percussionist.

"Alright, our kid. Who's this twat?"

Noel steamrollered his way into the band just as Liam knew he would. He changed every aspect of it: the clothes they wore, the songs they wrote. He changed the band name to that of a leisure centre. He wrote a batch of new songs that were loud, hedonistic and clumsy, but people seemed to like them. They were immediate, they were catchy, they swaggered, and they were extremely loud. Eventually, and having turned his attention to everything else, Noel turned his gaze on Liam, cornering him one day in the rehearsal room before the others got there. Liam was perched on an amp, poring over the Penguin edition of *The Eye* by Nabokov. He wore a peacoat, a black woollen rollneck, tapered needlecord trousers and black, suede Chukka boots. He sipped nervously on an imported Karelia cigarette.

"It's got to stop, son."

Liam looked up. "Hello, brother-mine. What's got to stop?"

"This. You."

"How do you mean? I am as God made me."

Noel scowled. "How'd you work that out? Look at you—got up like some left bank . . . *flaneur*. I've news for you, pal, it ain't the *rive gauche*, it's the *rive . . . go fuck yourself*."

"Bravo. As ever *le mot juste*."

"I'm serious. It's not the eighties—nobody wants mardy faced intellectual pop singers, fuckin' *Momus*. The nineties are going to be loud and it's going to be lairy and it's going to bring the people together."

"Even the idiots?"

"Especially them. Who do you think has the money?"

"But they don't even like bands. They don't go to gigs."

"They will," said Noel, "we'll make 'em. We'll cram ourselves down their throats till they're gagging for us. But you . . . look, if you wanna be part of this band you need to be more aggressive, louder and less . . . Paul fucking Morley. Here, I've brought you some clothes. Put these on."

He threw a bundle of clothes at Liam's feet.

"I don't understand. Are we going fishing?"

"That's what you're going to be wearing. If you don't like it, you're out of the band."

"But it's *my* band."

Noel snorted. "Not anymore, son. Not anymore."

Liam stamped his cigarette on the cement floor and threw down his paperback. He drew himself to his full height, towering over his brother by a full inch. This usurper, this mountebank, he had stolen into Liam's world of truth and beauty and coarsened it, replacing Liam's carefully metred poetry for nursery rhyme doggerel, his sophisticated, ironic worldview for rabble-rousing hyperbole, and now he was trying to change the way Liam dressed and even how he sang. Liam felt himself filling with emotion and, as inarticulate waves of pain and anger choked him, he struggled to voice his outrage at the vicissitudes raining down on him.

"It's a kerazy sit-choo-aaaation." He screamed, voice cracking.

Noel nodded. "Yeah, do it like that. You've got something there. "

Liam rose from his dressing table and wandered into his library. On the walls were prints by Odilon Redon and *The Ghost of a Flea* by William Blake. On the furthest wall from the window, away from the sunlight and under glass was an original oil painting: Felicien Rops' *Pornokrates*. It depicted a naked young girl in a blindfold leading a pig on a leash. As an image it spoke to Liam, and no matter how depressed he was he could always come into this room, with its rich leather scent, and stare at this painting and smile. He ran his fingers over the bookshelves and his hand came to rest on a paperback. It was creased and well-thumbed, the cover bright-red and featured the etiolated skeleton of a flower. This book had been the cornerstone of his miseducation. Like Dorian Gray's *Yellow Book*, it had opened him up to an exciting world of new possibilities, of stories, scents and sensations. The book fell open, and Liam read a few lines from *The Charm of Innocence*, nodding and smiling, before shutting it with a clap.

He peered out the window. The press was out there, one or two now, not like the nineties, but enough for him to put on the show. He slinked into his dressing room and set about the transformation, placing his silk dressing gown on a hanger. He put on an Ampro hoodie and shorts, and a pair of Novesta Shoes Star Masters in military green, because it was nice to give something back. Finally, he took the wig from the life-size phrenology head that rested on the lacquered surface of his dressing table. He smoothed it into place, teasing it at the edges, fussing with it, twisting individual hairs with saliva until he was satisfied. He stood still in front of the mirror, jutting his jaw and bending his legs. His arms hung at his sides, almost to the knee. He was ready to meet his public. Do it for the money, Liam. There was a Gustave Moreau painting coming up at auction. Think of that.

He opened the front door, flicked some Vs and gobbed on his own doormat. In a flurry of good-natured invective, he bowled his way down the street, cameras snapping at his heels.

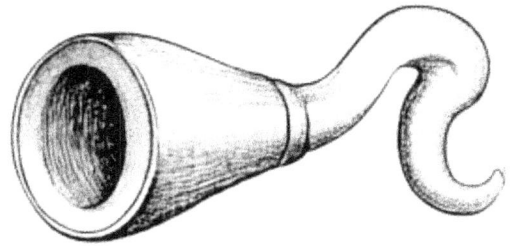

Roberta Allen

Four Wise Women Who Were Not Always Wise

The Wise Woman of Merema

The cave dwellers of Merema were known as the Special Ones because they had been chosen to live in a large subterranean cavern deep within the earth. Before they were chosen, the Special Ones had been as ordinary as everybody else.

Though they were living in what some islanders called Hell, the Special Ones didn't mind the dark, damp, airless underground chamber—or so they told themselves.

Everyone knew of the Wise Woman who had lived there for many years, but no one knew how she had chosen the Special Ones. Many non-specials believed they had been chosen at random.

But why choose anyone at all?

Maybe she's lonely, they told one another. Maybe she needs the presence of other human beings. But no one knew for sure.

Despite the conditions in the cave, the non-specials envied the Special Ones. They felt left out. They felt they weren't good enough. At the same time, the non-specials couldn't understand how anyone—special or not—could live without complaint amongst millipedes, beetles, mites, wood lice, spiders, cockroaches, eyeless amphibians, scorpions with venomous claws, and cave boas, not to mention the colony of roosting bats that numbered in the millions.

The bats tolerated the Wise Woman living there, but the presence of all those Special Ones in *their* cave was too much. One night while the Wise Woman slept, the bats made off with her cat's paw amulet. This should not have affected the amulet's function. The Wise Woman had uttered the proper incantations so the Special Ones would remain forever special, but something had gone wrong.

The Special Ones began complaining. The novelty of being special began to wear thin.

This is impossible! she told herself. But when she thought about it, she wondered if the amulet had become too weak after many years of use.

Soon she heard nothing but complaints.

The Special Ones admitted to each other that the dampness had seeped into the marrow of their bones. The darkness depressed them. They found the crawling and flying creatures *disgusting.* One after another, the Special Ones left the cave. The non-specials tried not to laugh as they watched them emerge. They were just like everybody else again. But they felt ashamed. They had given up. Nevertheless, it did not take long to see relief on their faces as their eyes adjusted to sunlight and they breathed in the clean fresh air.

The Wise Woman of Alotura

Overrun by rabid hog-nosed skunks, rabid horseshoe bats and red foxes planted by the Pusia people, their enemies, the Cabanese on the island of Caban were forced to flee their beloved island. Until then, the Cabanese had led peaceful lives. Happy lives. Of course, at times they felt fear, anger, grief, sadness just like everybody else, but they never wallowed in their feelings—unlike their enemies.

The Pusia were jealous of their happiness. But happiness is not a *forever* thing. It is, in fact, fleeting. Fragile. More fragile than even the Cabanese suspected. Until their enemies forced them to flee, the Cabanese did not know how fragile happiness is.

Should the Cabanese have fought their enemies? The Cabanese were not fighters. They had never had to defend themselves.

Perhaps if the Cabanese had been able to talk with their enemies, they could've taught them how to be happy. But their enemies were not interested in talking and in truth the Cabanese did not know if happiness was teachable.

Of course, by the time the Cabanese reached the shores of Alotora, they were anything but happy. In fact, they were too unhappy to go any further. Alotora was a beautiful island, but they couldn't see the emerald hills or the electric red wildflowers in the fields. Even the brightest blue sky was gray to them. The unhappiness inside themselves had seeped into the land, the water and the sky.

Everything was gray.

They now knew how their enemies felt.

The Cabanese were disappointed in the Wise Woman, but not as disappointed as she was in herself until one day while walking in the fields, she stumbled upon something small and pink by her feet. She bent down. It was palm size and oval shaped with a porcelain-like luster. It was too large to be a Queen Conch Pearl. Wasn't it? And what was it doing in a field? She picked it up. It vibrated in her hand. Was it alive? If so, it was not alive in the way she had known other things to be alive. Whatever it was, it called to her in what she later told the others was both *more* and *less* than a voice.

Holding it, she felt her unhappiness lift.

For the first time, she was able to *see* Alotora in all its beauty. *I was meant to find this!* she told herself. Excited, she told the others, "I have found a cure for our unhappiness!" She placed the pearl on top of a very large flat stone in the center of their makeshift village and told them all they must touch it every day.

"How do you know this?" they asked.

"There is a Spirit speaking through me," she told them. What else could it be?

Unknown to the Cabanese, a rabid red fox had stowed away on one of their boats. It had been watching them for some time. One night while they slept, it silently approached the stone, grabbed it and ran off. Sensing something was wrong, the Wise Woman awoke. Though she could not see it, the Spirit called to her again. Soon she found herself running down a long winding path at a speed that was far beyond anything she thought possible. When she saw the rabid fox up ahead fast approaching the boats where he might have hidden himself again, she uttered a scream so loud and otherworldly she could not believe her vocal cords had produced such a sound. Terrified, the fox dropped the pearl and continued running but it was so disoriented it began running in circles until it finally dropped in exhaustion and died.

Next day when the Cabanese rose and found the pearl on top of the large flat stone as usual, the Wise Woman did not tell them what had transpired. She did not know if next time she would be able to intervene on their behalf. She only knew there would be a next time, but she was not sure when that next time would be.

The Wise Woman of Baokkan

Andrew was the jealous type. When he saw how smitten Doreen was with Fred, he decided to put an end to it. Fred's voice was jewel-like, liquid, as smooth as molten silver. With that voice he had seduced nearly every female on the island of Baokkan. Doreen, his fiancé, was one of the few who had not yet succumbed only because Fred had not yet focused his attention on her. But Andrew knew it was only a matter of time. His Uncle Nate was the leader of a small clan best known for *disappearing* their rivals in the village square while everyone watched. How the clan was able to do this no one knew, but when Andrew went to see him and urgently explained his situation, Uncle Nate promised to *disappear* Fred's voice.

For two nights Fred dreamt about the sea.

The same dreams over and over.

When he awoke on the third day, his voice was gone. Fred was certainly not an exemplary Baokkian citizen, but the females he had seduced banded together angrily shouting, "Give Fred back his voice!"

Their memories kept them enamored. Otherwise, Fred was ordinary.

Though no one had seen the Wise Woman in recent years and almost everyone had forgotten her, Fred was frantic and descended to her underground cave, relieved to find her there. Since she was not only wise but a mind reader, she was able to see his thoughts.

Can you help me get my voice back?

"Where do you think it is?"

I keep dreaming about the sea.

"You think your voice is in the sea?"

Yes!

From her collection of amulets, she chose a fossilized limestone shell. "Maybe this will help," she said.

The shell felt cold at first.

Can you take me to the sea?

Before Fred could clear his throat properly, he was transported to the edge of a steep cliff, the sea below. He looked down, terrified. He had never learned to swim.

Trembling, he asked, *Shall I jump?*

Fred felt a gentle nudge, then jumped.

Confused and scared, he smacked the water hard, then descended hundreds of feet until the ocean floor was visible. Quickly, his eyes adjusted to the semidarkness. Surprising himself, he was suddenly swimming and without fear, but he was still confused. Jutting from the ocean floor, he saw giant stone-like mounds and creatures he never imagined.

What am I looking at?

The Wise Woman speaking through the amulet said, "Brain Coral, Pillar coral, Star coral—"

Is my voice hidden in one of those corals?

Silence.

On his own, Fred followed one creature after another, but they swam too fast or disappeared in the sand or hid like the moray eels under coral ledges.

Is my voice under one of those ledges?

Instead of answering him, the Wise Woman showed him parrotfish grazing on algae, anemones with stinging tentacles and sponges.

Is my voice here?

Silence.

Instead, the Wise Woman pointed out crayfish, lobsters, and shrimps living in nooks and crannies of the coral. Nearby an octopus emerged from the sand and changed color—

Is one of these creatures hiding my voice? Has the octopus buried it?

Silence.

He paused. *Why aren't you answering me?*

Fred watched Groupers over three feet long change from dark to light, then the giant eyes of several squids distracted him, then a coral crab crushing a sea urchin. Barracuda with razor sharp teeth hurried by, followed by jellyfish, transparent and umbrella-shaped, then sea fans and whips before he glimpsed a dull gray shark round a hard coral and schools of colorful striped and dotted fish—

Fred was awed but he was also exasperated. *Is my voice down here? Or is this just a wild goose chase?*

Again, silence.

Slowly, Fred rose from the depths, wondering whether his dreams were a sadistic joke played on him by the Wise Woman or by Uncle Nate. When he climbed up the steep cliff, Fred saw her at the top standing on the precipice from which he had jumped. When he was close enough, he handed her the amulet. Angry and disappointed, he said, *I don't believe my voice is there at all!*

"I knew you wouldn't find it," said the Wise Woman, sadly.

So why did you let me go?

"I had no choice. Uncle Nate and his clan threatened to take away my powers if I didn't take away your voice. I don't think they know how to do that, but I didn't want to take any chances. If I lost my powers and the powers of my amulets, I couldn't live. I'm so ashamed of everything I've done for Uncle Nate and the clan. That's why I haven't shown my face. But I see now it's better not to live at all than live corrupted by Uncle Nate and the clan."

With that, she stepped forward, toes over the edge.

Wait! At least give me back my voice before you jump! Fred shouted, suddenly aware of his own silvery sounds louder than he'd ever heard them before.

The Wise Woman of Yanap

The Wise Woman on the island of Yanap was tired of watching the unending misery of all the inhabitants on the island of Umbas. The unmarried, the married, the divorcees, the widows and widowers, the rich, the poor, the old, the young, even children did nothing but cry and complain. They lost friends and relations over trivial things. They lied about their income. They cheated on their spouses. They stole out of greed. Arguments often led to violence. Still, everyone lied, everyone cheated, everyone stole.

The Wise Woman knew the plants were the cause.

The poisonous plants.

The plants with their broad green leaves and delicate veins had poisoned the minds of the Umbasites. The scent, the seeds, the spores were enough to turn them into pitiful beings. If only she could rid the island of the plants. They were everywhere. But the island of Umbas was a week away from Yanap by boat. The sea between the islands was treacherous with rip tides, sharks, jellyfish with deadly stings and rogue waves swelling to impossible heights.

The Wise Woman dreamt of sending a group of happy islanders from Yanap—and they were *all* happy—to Umbas to show the Umbasites what happiness looks like and in so doing weaken the power of the plants. But she was a realist. It was far more likely that the plants would poison the Yanapese—if their boat was not smashed to smithereens first.

The Wise Woman rarely used her hag stone amulet, but she felt she had to do something, though she feared the distance from Yanap to Umbas was too great for the power of the hag stone. Even if it worked, its power might dissi-pate or produce unexpected results. Still, she thought it was worth a try. She held the amulet in her hand till it grew hot, very hot, rubbed it three times and sent its power across the sea.

Then she waited.

And waited.

At last, the Wise Woman watched the power of the hag stone amulet kill all the poisonous plants which ended the misery of the Umbasites. It stopped the islanders from living the life they lived but it left them with no life at all. The Wise Woman told them how disappointed she was, but the Umbasites were not disappointed. Though life was no longer an option, they considered what they had now in its place—whatever it was—to be better than anything they'd ever had before.

SHya ScanLon

An American Story

At first a discrete measure to afford his old dog's mounting medical costs, Doug's foray into amateur porn had now matured into a prolonged strategic campaign. This alone would have made the summer memorable, but then he fell in love. Come to think of it, though, maybe "fell" wasn't quite accurate. He and Mary had barely known one another before deciding to cohabitate, and perhaps because of the ostensibly transactional nature of their relationship his feelings had been slow to deepen—not a falling at all, then, so much as a long decline. Happily, the path he'd taken to get there did nothing in its lack of urgency to lessen the power of his arrival. The love was real. He'd never been so sure of anything in his life. Doug stood at the kitchen window to watch a protest pass by three stories below. Then Mary texted him from her bedroom. It was 2:00 pm. Time for the sex act.

After a livestream show, they'd often drape their pale bodies across the bed and have a post-coital chat with their fans, and they did so that afternoon too. It had turned into a little community of sorts, their only stable social life. They'd share videos and memes, talk about their pets. Occasionally, Doug would even forget why they were all there to begin with. Someone with the screen-name PigMental was talking about Pornhub's new privacy settings when Doug remembered that he had an important announcement to make.

"I have an important announcement to make," he said.

Mary frowned.

"Tomorrow we've got a special show for you! Be sure to tune in."

Mary looked to the screen, and when fans began to signal their enthusiasm in the chat she softened. "Same bat time, same bat place, you perverts," she said, and cupped her breasts.

After they stopped the livestream she admonished him for surprising her on camera, but Doug could sense a hint of amusement.

"So what, finally gonna let me peg you?"

"You'll find out tomorrow."

Mary shoved him, a bit playfully, a bit not.

"Come on. Let it be a surprise? Please?"

She rolled off the bed and made for the bathroom. "You're making dinner."

Doug and Mary had been set up by a common friend at the beginning of the year. They'd gone on a few dates and had liked one another well enough, but it wasn't sparking anything for either of them. They were parting amicably when the pandemic hit, and in short order Mary's roommate had moved back to Ohio and Doug's restaurant had shut its doors. The city was closing down. She invited him to move in. She was opinionated, easy to talk to, and cool with his fifteen-year-old Boston Terrier, Fetch, who his parents had hoisted on him five years ago when he'd graduating college. They stopped trying to make Fetch happen, Mary had said. Doug had had to look it up.

Fetch seemed fine until he wasn't, and then he was bad. Soon after they moved in with Mary his hind legs stopped working right and he began to lose bladder control. Doug spent much of his meager savings just getting a diagnosis, and when he was told surgery would be needed to remove a tumor pressing against the dog's spine, he thought that was that. But Mary'd had another idea. Toward the end of March she'd sent him a link to her Pornhub channel, where she'd been posting a series of solo videos under the moniker QuaranTeen. She was thirty, five years older than Doug, but she could still basically pull it off by wearing ponytails. Doug was shocked and aroused. How had he not known this? Their bedrooms were at opposite ends of the apartment, but how had he not heard?

Mary said that she was making good money, and that together they could make more than double. "That's where you come in."

"So to speak."

"I trust you'll be professional about this."

O ver dinner, Mary scrolled through fan mail while Doug read. He'd been finding it increasingly difficult to sustain interest across an entire book by a single author, but he could stomach anthologies. The lottery of it kept him going. Just then he was reading *New American Stories*, edited by Ben Marcus, and was on a George Saunders short called "Home." It was the second within the first third of the book set against the backdrop of war. With the pandemic raging and Black Lives Matter protests burning through cities across the country, war seemed to Doug like an exotic concern, but Saunders handled it the same way he handled any topic, which is to

say gracefully and with self-effacing humor. "Home" wasn't his strongest effort, but it had all the hallmarks of the author's best work: the brisk dialogue, the dim-witted characters, the way those two elements would occasionally combine into hilariously broken grammar like, "It's been many a day since I reclined in a nice place of that nature such as a hotel." His was a world, it occurred to Doug, in which big flaws were worn openly because everything was finally forgiven. Despite his focus on people without much to lose, Saunders was an optimist. Which was probably why his work felt anachronistic.

Mary put down her phone. "What are you reading?"

He showed her the cover. Mary was exceedingly well-read. From the start she'd not only have already read everything he mentioned, she'd be able to explain why it fell short. She was like an Amazon recommendation engine of contempt. He'd hated this at first, but over time he'd come to understand that his initial response was just dumb ego, something that ought to be properly exposed. It was now one of the things he loved most about her.

"That's a pretty good antho," Mary said. "I mean, not as good as the Anchor one he did a decade before. He kind of lost his edge."

Doug's heart swelled.

He looked up the title she mentioned and scanned the table of contents. "To be fair," he said, "there's a lot of overlap. George Saunders, Deborah Eisenberg, Anthony Doerr . . . Do you think that's as in 'door' or like Dürrenmatt?"

"Let me see."

"Christine Schutt. Sam Lipsyte."

She grabbed his phone.

"Yeah but I mean, Anne Carson? Gary Lutz? Diane Williams? Brilliant. Deeply weird-in-a-good-way. None of them in the newer book."

"Wells Tower," he said.

Mary wandered into her bedroom and Doug spent a bit more time with the *Anchor* TOC. It occurred to him that it was a whiter list. There was Jhumpa Lahiri. The only other writer who wasn't your standard white American was Alexander Hemon, and despite being an ethnic minority, Hemon was white as hell. Not that the newer book did much better on this front. Out of thirty-two authors, six were minorities. Maybe seven. Doug didn't have the energy to Google them all. Anyway, Mary would completely dress him down for bringing this stuff up. To her, literature was a pure meritocracy, or should be. Political correctness would kill it. Just a few weeks earlier, *Harper's* had published an open letter decrying cancel culture that was signed by a laundry list of cultural elite from Martin Amis to Margaret Atwood—Mary had been outraged by the outrage that had followed. She found it self-evident that in a climate where people were forced to police their own thoughts, we'd end up blunting our own imaginations.

"People want to be spoon fed like babies," she'd said. "It's condescending and gross."

Doug had suggested that perhaps Martin Amis was being a bit thin-skinned. Surely he could handle a small correction to his value in the market of ideas.

Mary ignored him. "I doubt Salman Rushdie ever imagined he'd have to defend his right to free speech in the very societies who'd helped him defend it during the fatwa. The mind reels."

Sirens wailed outside, and Fetch, scared of everything, hobbled into the room to tremble. Tumor and riots notwithstanding, Fetch probably loved quarantine. His people around all the time. Nonstop pets. He'd never been into other dogs, so not getting dragged to the park was A-okay. But something not great had been happening with Doug re man's best friend. Even though the surgery, done in June, had mitigated Fetch's disability and, hopefully, pain, Doug had become increasingly put off by the dog. Since the operation Fetch had become paranoid, needy. They'd put him on Prozac, which helped a little but not enough. He incessantly followed Doug around the apartment, always underfoot, and Doug had to fight the urge to kick him. Mary said that it was all about preparation for Fetch's death, that Doug was distancing himself out of a need for self-protection. Maybe this was true, but it made him feel like shit nonetheless, which feelings made him resent the poor dog even more. He'd spent all this money to prolong Fetch's life, only to spend the time he'd bought wishing the dog were dead.

"Okay dummy," he said, lifting Fetch off the floor.

Fifteen years ago, Fetch had been the result of a doomed romantic gesture. His high school girlfriend had seen him listed at a kill shelter, too old to be easily placed, and he'd secretly pleaded with his parents to adopt. The plan was to bring him to college—they'd both gotten into State—and share custody in the off-campus dorms. On graduation day, he'd surprised her with Fetch, and she'd surprised him with the fact that she'd gotten into a better school. She'd quickly broken things off, but he'd held out hope that she'd change her mind and choose him, choose them. By the time he found out that State didn't allow pets anyway Fetch was part of the family. So he'd pleaded with his parents again.

Fetch squirmed until Doug put him down. "Et tu?" He cleared the table.

Anthologies were easy to consume, but all the stories started to blend together—even while you were still reading. To fight this, Doug had been experimenting with a simple mnemonic. He gave each story a series of three words or phrases that had a distinct meaning for the text, words that when recited brought the whole story to mind, its mood, its settings, its language and pivotal moments. Like for "The Deep" by Anthony Doerr, he'd chosen the words salt, heart, and amphibian. Rebecca Lee's "Slatland" could be summoned with fear, Romania, and girliewhirl. The story he'd read last was "Shhhh," by NoViolet Bulawayo.

"Family, AIDS, Find bin Laden," Doug said.

Mary poked her head into the room. "You say something?"

"I'm working on my memory."

Though anthologized as American, the NoViolet Bulawayo story felt "African" in ways that were hard to describe. It had something to do with the playful patois, the witch doctors and poverty. It took place in Zimbabwe, which was the author's birth country, where English was one of the official languages. Bulawayo had probably always spoken it. So the story hadn't been translated, but there'd been a more fundamental translation: that of the author. She'd translated herself from Zimbabwe to Texas, from

Texas to Cornell. In 2011 she'd won the Caine Prize for African Writing, and yet here she was.

Another story, "A Man Like Him," by Yiyun Li, was also written about the culture of her birth country, in this case China. Wikipedia called Yiyun Li a "Chinese writer"—Doug supposed because that was still her citizenship, but wasn't sure.

Would these stories still be considered American if they weren't written in English? What if they weren't written in the United States? What was an American story? Judging by this collection, it seemed to Doug, one thing it certainly was: a wandering series of lightly acerbic, aw-shucks encounters that began and ended *in media res*. Eisenberg, Antrim, Johnson. Especially Johnson. Williams and DeLillo. Tower, Gaitskill, Watkins. You just plugged in your idiosyncratic interests, sprinkled in wry observations, and leaned on privilege—years as an exchange student, a bachelor's degree in mineralogy, familiarity with New York literati—and presto: American fiction. He loved these authors dearly, but it was as though the nation's default posture was a dumbfounded disbelief that it had come to this, a bashful, almost embarrassed admission that we'd all made it through alive. Both Yiyun Li and NoViolet Bulawayo broke from that mold in different but equally obvious ways. Despite being vastly different writers, their work had an earnestness in common that a lot—not all, but a lot—of the other stories in the collection lacked. It couldn't have been incidental that both these authors were astonishingly accomplished, having earned, in a country they'd adopted, the highest degrees from the most prestigious institutions. There was something distinctly American about that, too. Was it their drive, their force of will, that helped them shed the breezy air of so much fiction written by their white American counterparts? They'd made it through, but their characters still hadn't. The sirens subsided and Doug took the relative quiet as a chance to walk Fetch.

As usual, it was eerie outside. Traffic was scarce, and everyone either made dramatic gestures of giving one another space, or else made equally dramatic gestures of refusing to. After college, Doug had moved to the city to become a writer. He'd quickly found the right places to be, a community of strivers like himself that busied themselves with the work of climbing the ladder built by those who'd come before. They'd started magazines and published one another's work. They'd created reading series. They'd fucked and gossiped. There'd been an expectation that they'd all eventually succeed in one way or another and Doug had shared this expectation, but somehow his energy always felt a little misplaced. How should the lower rungs of a ladder feel about being instrumental to the success of those who manage to reach the top? Anyway, there was still time. He turned down a street that was literally empty for an entire block and watched Fetch sniff around for a place to shit—a process that had become increasingly labor intensive.

He texted Mary, "Would you Like this tweet: Most people think toilets are about sanitation, but any dog walker would confirm that they're mostly about taking the guesswork out of finding the right place to do your business."

Bubbles formed immediately, and within a few seconds Mary's reply came in. "TLDR how about: My dog says toilets aren't for keeping clean. They're for making it easy to find the right place to poop."

"Yeah, better."

Mary texted again. "Hey, I'm looking for a book. Can I go in your room?"

"Oh, actually, please don't! Could ruin surprise."

"WTF"

"BRB"

Doug hurried home.

The ring was probably in the back of his sock drawer, but maybe he'd left it out? He'd been unable to resist marveling at it two or three times a day so who knew. When Doug was safely in his room with the door closed he felt a flood of relief, but instead of letting Mary in he took the ring out, sat at his small desk, and opened the brown leather box to do more marveling. The ring was modest but, he hoped, classic, a platinum band holding Mary's birthstone, a ruby. Though she hadn't mentioned it, he knew from stalking her rarely checked Facebook account that it would in fact be her birthday the very next day: July 20th.

He'd gone to great lengths to get the size right, printing out a paper ring sizer and sneaking into her room while she was out to use it on a ring he'd seen her wear on the right finger. Tomorrow he'd present the box on one knee in front of their fans on the livestream channel before or after making love—he hadn't decided—in what was surely the most insane and romantic proposal in the history of marriage proposals. In his mind he'd told her this story a hundred times in the future they shared, trying out comic exaggerations, teasing it out. They were older. They'd settled down. She'd stare into his eyes on their fifth, their tenth, their fiftieth anniversary and ask him to tell it to her again. It was insane. He knew it was insane. There was nothing to do but go through with it. He heard a scratch at the door. He'd forgotten about Fetch.

As 2:00 pm drew near the next day, Doug grew anxious. Everything had to be perfect. He'd somehow managed to *plan* for this without actually *preparing*, and he was having trouble accessing that thrillingly naïve excitement he'd had for days on end. He'd had it just the day before! Where had it gone? He thought of the fans who'd be tuning in from all over the world. Attendance for their livestreams varied, but there were a good two dozen regulars, and he was hoping for a big turnout. In retrospect it was amazing to him how quickly he'd developed a kind of intimacy with these people who paid cash money to watch him and Mary fuck. In most cases, he didn't know what they looked like—he didn't even know their real names. But they'd worn his defenses down in a war of attrition. Whereas at first he'd felt judged under the harsh literal daylight of their staged performance, he'd quickly begun to feel encouraged. And day after day, week after week, lifting upward from the platform of that encouragement, he'd finally begun to feel loved.

Doug lay on his bed beside Fetch. It was exceptionally noisy outside that afternoon and the dog was shivering in fear. It was the "Strike for Black Lives;" thousands of workers considered essential had walked off the job. Mary seemed irritable, which sucked. He tried to distract himself, couldn't concentrate, ended up reciting story mnemonics.

"Some Other, Better Otto" by Deborah Eisenberg: family, resentment, denial.

"Another Manhattan" by Donald Antrim: desperation, love, denial.

"The Country" by Joy Williams: Tank, paperclip, denial.

So, there were some patterns.

The first story in the collection was called "Paranoia," written by a Brooklyn native named Saïd Sayrafiezadeh. It was about a relationship between two young men, maybe in their twenties. One was a white guy with a good job, the other an illegal immigrant from south of the border. It was written from the white guy's perspective, and covered a city summer where record temperatures blanket everything in oppressive heat. Jobs are scarce, and there's a war about to happen somewhere, though that's mostly off camera. It's just felt looming at the edges of the frame. The narrator cares for his immigrant friend, but he also clearly looks down on him. He helps him, but also seems to believe he's beyond help. Then one day the INS comes and takes the immigrant away. And that's it. Like the war, the meaning of the story seemed to exist at the periphery of this small relationship, this fragile, imperfect bond that stood against all odds.

The text finally came in from Mary. It was time for the sex act.

"Fetch, wish me luck."

He gripped the ring box tightly as he made his way down the hall. The outside noise grew louder as he approached Mary's room, and upon entering he saw the reason: her window was open, and she was leaning halfway out. She was topless. Her hair was in ponytails. There were cheers from down below, but then she began shouting.

"Go back home!" she called. "Some of us have work to do!"

The crowd quickly turned on her, and Doug heard a bottle break against the side of the building. He asked her to come back inside but she ignored him.

"Fuck you!" she screamed, and then, "Did you see that? Did you see that!?"

Doug pressed his forehead against the glass and looked down to see a pair of police officers on horseback, one looking up at Mary, the other speaking into a radio at his shoulder. For a moment Doug wondered what they thought they were seeing. A teen? A sexy teen vixen held hostage by her parents? But then they moved on. QuaranTeen was not their concern. The march kept marching and Doug squeezed Mary's waist, a reminder. It was nearly two. They had a show to put on and he had marriage to propose. She lingered at the window as though lost in thought, and he had a heady sensation of déjà vu. If his summer was an American story, what mnemonic would help him remember it? Love, obviously. Love and porn. He tried to think of a third word, something that could conjure the gritty, specific texture of this strange chapter of his life—a turning point, after all, maybe a climax—a word that might triangulate the hedonism of the first two with pathos, but the interminable chanting outside the open window filled his ears and drowned out his thoughts.

Dan Morey

Snigglefritz Flies

The students are listening to Alex Ross read, when Snigglefritz walks in. He's wearing a polka-dot onesie with a yellow ruff and pointy dunce cap. His face is caked with white makeup, but there's no red rubber nose. Snigglefritz doesn't do red rubber noses.

Professor Cowboy jingles his spurs and says, "You're late again, Fritz."

The students grumble. Alex Ross is particularly annoyed—he was halfway through his story, and his delivery had been perfect.

Snigglefritz says, "Late? I better do da pee test!" He puffs out his stomach in a parody of pregnancy, and honks his squeeze horn twice. Honk! Honk!

"Not yer best stuff, Fritz," says Professor Cowboy. "Take a seat."

Snigglefritz clomps over to an empty desk, flapping his shoes loudly. Honk!

"Can I please resume my story now?" says Alex Ross.

"Let 'er rip," says Professor Cowboy.

As Alex Ross reads, the students entertain various individual thoughts.

Derek Longhair: I'd like to smoke pot when I get home, but I'd also like to conjugate Latin verbs. Can these activities be done simultaneously?

Ben From Wisconsin: Is it okay to wear overalls in the city?

Dan Morey: In the third set, when I had that break point, why didn't I go down the line on the return? Why?

Lady Charlotte: These Americans are awful. I wish I were rowing on the Thames.

Colonel Vargas: I respect Alex Ross's visor, but I would not wear such a visor myself.

Snigglefritz: I belong on the trapeze. Flying free. Why do I degrade myself like this?

Meiny: Naked ladies, naked ladies, naked ladies.

Alex Ross finishes reading, and Professor Cowboy awakens with a snort. "Boots!" he says. "Who stole my boots?"

Derek Longhair says, "That was a very well-written story, but the stakes seem kind of low."

"It's a language piece," says Alex Ross. "I hate stakes."

"So do I," says Dan Morey.

"Me too," says Snigglefritz. "Especially New York Strip." Honk! Honk!

The students groan. Meiny says, "I think there's too much telling in the narration, and not enough showing."

"You want a show, big boy?" says Snigglefritz. "Take-a-looka-dis!" He stands up, turns around, and pulls down his trouser flap. There's a rubber buttocks inside. Honk! Honk!

Professor Cowboy removes his hat, and patiently adjusts the feathers. "Yer in rare form today, Fritz, but we've got work to do. Sit the hell down."

Honk!

Lady Charlotte says, "I'm afraid the ending of Alex Ross's story just didn't resonate with me."

Snigglefritz whips out a plastic vibrator. "Try dis, lady!" Buzzzzz. Honk! Honk!

"Oh, brother," says Ben From Wisconsin. "How much did I pay for this class?"

When the workshop is over, the students go outside and sit around the sunken garden. Professor Cowboy mounts his horse and rides off across campus.

"That horse has a very fine gallop," says Colonel Vargas. "But I do not like its canter."

"If you knew Susie, like I know Susie . . ." sings Snigglefritz, doing a little shuffle. The students glare at him. Insects chirp. "Eddie *Cantor*!" he says.

"Yeah," says Meiny. "Let's hit the sports bar. Later, Fritz."

The students abandon Snigglefritz on a bench among the rose bushes. Other young people pass by in merry groups, shoving each other, giggling, shouting Victor Hugo quotes. As darkness descends, Snigglefritz gives his horn a weak squeeze and hums a few bars from *Pagliacci*.

At the sports bar, Dan Morey drinks too many Grand Slam Cocktails and wanders across the street to the Furama Hotel. He is soon ejected from the lounge for starting a loud argument over who makes better tennis balls, Penn or Slazenger.

Lady Charlotte is standing on a table in the sports bar, singing "Down at the Old Bull and Bush," when they get the news about Dan Morey. She orders another round of port, and says, "It's most unfortunate. Should we see him home?"

"Let him sleep on the tennis court," says Alex Ross.

"Now, now," says Derek Longhair.

"I don't like Dan Morey," says Alex Ross. "He's always stealing my characters. And he wrote a poem about me having sex with birds."

"He is a good tennis player," says Colonel Vargas, adjusting her epaulettes. "But he will never be great."

Ben From Wisconsin says, "I wish he'd go home and shower before coming to class. He smells worse than a farmhand after four hours of hay pitching, and I'm always tripping over his racquet bag."

"At least he's better than Snigglefritz," says Meiny, tossing back his third tumbler of Malört.

"Ugh," says Ben From Wisconsin. "Snigglefritz. How'd he get into this school, anyway?"

Derek Longhair says, "The dean heard him reciting limericks at a rodeo in Sacramento. He was very impressed."

"Bullshit," says Meiny. "He's a legacy. Fourth gen. His great-grandfather brought a circus over here from München, and funded the school's first library with Big Top money."

Alex Ross laughs, and takes a sip of spit-fermented masato. "You're both wrong. Snigglefritz transferred from a Clown College in Heidelberg. Word is he was close to flunking out."

"I don't doubt it with those jokes," says Lady Charlotte.

"Well, wherever he came from, we're workshopping his story next Tuesday," says Meiny. "We'll see what he's made of then."

Snigglefritz spends the following week at the fairgrounds, working tirelessly on his story. Except for his peppermint-striped tent, the fairgrounds are completely desolate, and he can write without distraction. For inspiration, he looks to his muse, the ghost of Vera Schwepps, famed circus equestrienne. Thanks to her, what began as a piece of flash fiction has now expanded to novella length.

Somewhere around page sixty, Snigglefritz senses that an ending is near, but just as he's about to wrap up the plot, Vera Schwepps enters the tent, dragging her bad leg across the dirt floor. She perished in a fire (set by Lilly LaPutia Codona, wife of Vera's Spanish paramour), and the leg isn't much more than bones and patches of gelatinous flesh.

"Don't stop now, Fritzie," she says, panting over his shoulder with rancid breath. "This yarn is just getting good."

Vera Schwepps contorts her face into a grim smile. Her skin is blue, her teeth charred black from the fire, and one of her pigtails has been gnawed off by burrowing vermin. Snigglefritz is enflamed with creative ecstasy. Words fly from his pen in a frenzy, seeming to compose themselves. He fills the last page of his notebook and immediately starts another.

The tale centers on Poodles, a lowly circus clown who longs to become a trapeze artist. Every night, he watches from the shadows as the renowned Colitis Cousins perform their graceful leaps and somersaults high above the ring. Oh, how he dreams of being up there, floating in the limelight. When one of the cousins is taken ill (soggy spleen syndrome), Poodles, who has been practicing on the trapeze during his off hours, is asked to fill in. Finally, he will have his chance to fly.

By the end of the week, Snigglefritz is exhausted. He glugs down a bottle of nerve tonic and collapses on his cot. As he drifts off, the wind picks up, blowing dust under the tent flaps, and sweeping in the ghost of Vera Schwepps. She squishes her eyeballs around their sockets so she can see straight, and says, "This is it, Fritzie. There's only one way the story can end. You know it and I know it. Now get off your rump and write it."

She limps out and climbs onto her phantom steed. Snigglefritz watches them depart, Vera Schwepps's lone pigtail twirling in the breeze.

O n the day of the workshop, Snigglefritz arrives on time, in his best Pierrot suit. He doesn't crack jokes or honk his horn. There is a single black teardrop painted under his right eye.

"Cheer up, Fritz," says Professor Cowboy. "This is supposed to be fun."

Snigglefritz begins to read—seriously, solemnly—and his listeners become more rapt with each sentence. Their thoughts vary.

Derek Longhair: It's like Greek tragedy.

Ben From Wisconsin: Cripes, this clown can write.

Dan Morey: He's crushing it, but can he serve it out?

Lady Charlotte: I'm resonating all over.

Colonel Vargas: He is bleeding on the page. Magnificent.

Alex Ross: Can't believe I'm thinking this, but Snigglefritz might be a genius.

Professor Cowboy: This sonofabitch is better than *me*.

Meiny: Too long, dude. Naked ladies.

When Snigglefritz finishes his story, the students are dumbstruck. Alex Ross's mouth hangs open like an astonished yokel. Lady Charlotte

faints. Colonel Vargas stands and salutes. Genuinely touched and on the verge of tears, Snigglefritz makes an elaborate bow, and exits.

T he university's literary awards ceremony is held at the end of the semester, and Snigglefritz takes top honors. Dan Morey comes in second with a story about a gorilla who learns to play tennis and goes on to win the mixed doubles championship at Wimbledon. Third place goes to Meiny for his poetry collection, *Odalisques*.

Dan Morey and Meiny are present to accept their awards, but Snigglefritz doesn't show. In fact, no one has seen him since the workshop. Concerned, Professor Cowboy rides out to the fairgrounds, and finds Snigglefritz's tent slumped in the middle of the field. The tent is empty, except for a desk. There's a note on it, pinned beneath a squeeze horn. It says, *Auf Wiedersehen*.

O ne year later, the students from Professor Cowboy's fiction workshop gather at a rustic tavern in a small town near Lückendorf, Saxony. Snigglefritz was laid to rest there after a horrific trapeze accident at a circus in the Sudetenland.

Lady Charlotte has donned a dirndl for the wake, and Meiny is clad in his grandfather's lederhosen. Dan Morey sports his favorite Tacchini tracksuit, Alex Ross a vintage Aloha shirt and matching visor. Derek Longhair has fashioned his coif into a respectful braid, while Colonel Vargas has polished her boots so that they gleam even in the gray winter light. There are a few circus people in attendance as well, but they keep mostly to themselves, playing lugubrious tunes on bent instruments.

"It's so sad," says Lady Charlotte. "Just like his story."

"Life imitating art," says Derek Longhair.

Dan Morey raises his bottle of kellerbier in a toast. "He could've been better than Heine. Better than Goethe. Hell, he could've beat Boris Becker in straight sets if he put his mind to it. But Snigglefritz didn't want to be the best. He just wanted to fly. Up above it all. If only for a brief moment. And he did! Here's to the flying clown. His words will live on."

Everyone at the long table taps glasses.

"Now let's get blotto!" says Meiny. He chugs a stein of dunkel and starts to dance, slapping his thighs maniacally. "Hey!" he yells at the circus people. "Any of you freaks got an accordion?"

A bald, muscled man in a leopard-print leotard produces a concertina and pumps away. Everyone dances. Later, the whole drunken gang stumbles out of the tavern into the dark village streets. Derek Longhair lights a torch and leads them up the hill to the burying ground. People in the houses along the way stare out their windows and extinguish lamps as the motley parade passes.

It's chilly, with flecks of snow in the air. Trees, leafless and skeletal, cast swaying shadows over the mossy tombstones. Students and circus people mingle at Snigglefritz's grave. Alex Ross puts his arm around Aviana the Bird Girl to warm her delicate body. Derek Longhair lowers the torch and reads out the epitaph:

"Here lies Snigglefritz the Wise. Another tragic clown. What a cliché. Honk. Honk."

RW Spryszak

Time Tables

Our train, a knife infinitely sharp, cuts through the tattered white lace fog careless on a bridge of sticks high above the ravine I strain to catch the unseeable bottom of and I recall that when the world was green I believed every lie they told me, even in the trinkets of their gods and the glory of their dead and I believed in these things hard until the day came when I believed in nothing and came to understand that I have endowed too many inanimate things with life and here I am, riding the homebound train because of the tethers and the expectations and the fate of all sons, wordless, speaking to no one, interested in no one, seeking time with no one on a church of a train working under the order of a catechism of timetables.

Unable to see the bottom of the ravine because of the fog and the distance and the short breath of time I turn my face from the cold window and watch her approach as if I was the only one to see her as she lifts her hands in delicate delicto, fingernails yellow from the grip of disease, a ripped tunic ballerina once lighter in those shoes a hundred years ago as she poses, watching her rancid body in the great mirror the fog outside makes of my window.

"See how I did it?" She trills. "They loved me. My friends. Champagne. Almonds. Children at my feet." Her arms raise to her sides like a penguin. "We didn't show the cracks and chips in those days. It would have destroyed the illusion." She holds her pose with her blue vein arms, a harrowing network of thinning rivers meandering beneath the remnants of what was once clean skin, her garment of old weeds a maze of hanging threads unwound by time and you can hear somewhere a jewelry box that opens and plays a chime of heraldry as the wires make the plastic dancer twirl, skipping where the gear is broken as the piano in the old dancer's head clinks tin notes as she lifts an imaginary leg.

I prefer the morphine of memory too, but mine are not as worn dead as hers, and remembrance does not become her with her breath a stale blue and her perfume barely covering the sweat of sick garlic, the stink of human promise as she makes a series of poses.

"Friends. Admirers. They came for me, you know. Some of the men offered the lewdest things." Her head begins to spin, possessed, but there isn't enough blood to force her face to blush.

"I can imagine," I reassure her faulty memory, humoring her madness.

"Would you like to buy an arabesque?" She goes to one leg but has to hold the other in her hands, waiting for my answer. "I am only charging sovereigns tonight."

"I do not believe in kings," I hear myself say but the sarcasm is missed because she can barely plié with those are ancient bones, brown from use and fire and there will be no tour en l'air.

"Nothing at all?"

I don't answer for reasons of my own because I don't want to be bothered, because I didn't invite her here, because we sleep on the ground once hallowed by the shamans we long ago burned at the stake as sorcerers and devils, because there's no such a thing as karma there is only irony, and she stops, seemingly insulted, as the mirror of my window made by the passing fog begins to dissipate, revealing a faint green shimmer of a house in the trees as the sun starts to obliterate the haze, and she drops her faulty posing as if I've ruined her entire dream.

I say "I take it the show is over then," and am immediately sorry for words that sound like a heckling taunt knowing full well I can be cruel that way, it's how I recognize myself, and she sulks away, broken, her emerald glow of what once was snuffed into powder and blown by the wind, returning to her seat where her friends, who have been watching all along, pat her shoulders and say comforting things while sneering in my direction wordlessly saying how can you be so heartless and I don't have an answer and I think how is it possible for her to have friends watching, saying nothing, letting her do that.

We move slow through the place she was born, a sordid scratch of roads that is no rural harbor, no farmland carnival, no safe haven with its motionless rain and dead birds in flat puddles because the people here are all gone or else looking to escape and she is the only one left on the platform as we roll once again, her friends still on the train as I watch her struggling with a suitcase twice her size and it becomes obvious to me that, like her, the world will end in a landslide of broken bones and things we can't lift anymore.

There are timetables to keep and we are moving into a tunnel as the warning whistle clears the dank black of the cavern of anything that's in the way because there are creatures in this tunnel, everybody knows, that have been lost for all time, never before seen by man, and sometimes they fall to the tracks in suicide surrender.

I will get off at the station at the foot of the far mountains by the sea but there are still miles to go and there is no point to watching the passing scene because I already know it by heart and I cover myself with a blanket and close my eyes though all I can see are the things I tell no one that live in my head where the places of sleep should be, knowing I will wake the next morning and not be rested but turned out hollow and dirty like an empty barrel or a dead saint.

And then, with my head pounding against the window at every roll of the car over the warping tracks, feeling the light outside the train, I pull the blanket from my face and see the sailing ships in the harbor so clear I can taste their famous old smells, hear the salt and sea and watch the gull's blue wing high above the clouds toward the hook of a moon that will soon be overcome with full daylight.

If I'd slept a little longer I would have learned to play the melody that went on and on in my half-sleep but instead I was home in my old town by the sea where sometimes, in the clutches of autumn, the searchers draw red stones from the water.

It's the only thing we're famous for.

Kevin Davey

Moon scythes night's swirl of grain

(From *Toothpull of St Dunstan*)

Dark dwellings impasto, rooves looming, eaves leaking shadow. Trees with braided branches, eel traps upended. I work the view standing.

—My hat's a crown with twelve candles.

The wagon of Margaret Roper is anticipated. As alerts the beadle, baits the hook.

—She'll reach for her purse alright. She's grieving.

He waits at her gate with a young assistant.

Hooves we hear, wheels on gravel. I snuff my candelarbre tiara, retreating indoors with the daub.

The dray mare pants, pollods in the pitch plods and nods to end the haul. The wagon waddles and lumps. I spy at the window.

Call on the driver to halt, the beadle bids the clerk. The wagon stops.

He circles it slowly, hawk inspecting prey. She knows the play. He swoops.

—What's in the baggage my lady?

—Clothing and books.

—Your father's goods?

—They were.

Chords of scent attract his beak. Discard offal, cherry musk. Rose and violets, butcher's waste. He thrusts his head about a covered basket on her lap. He snuffles, looks up at her, lays close and sniffs deeply.

—Vial of nosegay, cracked?

—It is not.

—I would know what the wicker holds. Take a look boy.

Hold hold she cries alarmed. She stays the clerk's hand. The boy looks to the beadle. She lets the arm drop. She speaks but faintly.

—My father's head.

—Haha. Very funny my lady. Open it lad.

The clerk places the basket in the road, in a pool of moonlight. He cuts the hemp binding. He lifts the lid. He raises a lump wrapped in swads of twill. He puts the obscurity beside the basket. He unwads it.

—Pray take care.

A skull.

—Ye gods!

A recent skull with cartilage and hair, flush with herbs. The woman Roper sobs.

Father.

AIYAI OHAI AIYAIA! an unearthly wailing sound from the cranium. Mumbling, tapping, an eggshell fracking.

My Dearest Meg clacks the nog, spitting leaf.

The clerk folds. He vomits loudly, a rank vegetal slop. The daughter drops to her knees. She looks on the pan of her father. Her eyes stream, stung by steam from the clerk's spew.

The skull looks on, helplessly. The beadle's brisk.

—Far side of the way if you need to lad. Take water from my saddle.

He turns to the daughter.

—From where does yon rottenness come? You've consents?

—None are needed. From London.

—Where specific in that smoke?

—The crossing at Southwark, the bridge.

Falling down is falling down cackles the pate, London bridge is falling down, mosh for joy. The skull rocks violently, scooping mire from the street.

Oh father, she warns with a whisper.

—Dullards dread satire, please don't.

The clerk retches again, draped over a low wall. Puke scalds his nose.

—Back on your feet lad. Stand up.

The beadle squats by the bone.

—The chapel of St Thomas on the bridge? From thence?

A most blessed place pipes the pate, nodding. The clackety chavyl sheds a tooth.

—No.

—So does your lady mean St Magnus? Or our Mary Overie?

—I do not.

—A knocking shop perhaps, prised from a whip?

—I'll say!

The skull bursts from its burrow, yes yes why not indeedy!

—No.

—Oh.

The brow lifts, the jaw chimes at the stars.

I'll be home tonight by the light of the silvery moon
Heart's thumpin a mandolin plunkin a tune

If you were a member of the London evangelical community, More was a deeply unpleasant proposition.

—You'd fear him, couldn't trust him, wouldn't think him holy.

—Certainly not a hero.

His skull swings up like a bell, pealing.

When I get home I'm fixin to stay
Whip-crack awa, whip-crack awa, whip crack
awa!

Exasperated, Lady Margaret interrupts.

—Enough! Father was pulled from a spike on the gate. He looked from there these four weeks last.

How went that the beadle asks.

Purgatory, laments the skull, a damnable spot.

—How so?

—Try it you'll see! Same scene every day, each day a repeat.

Stinking fish sellers sottish hop haulers foraging alchemists engrossers enclosers Anglican gloaters.

—More?

—Vainglorious Royals parasite abbots elegant usurers pedlars barbers overladen wagons smuggling stowaways ice boulders ice cream vans screamy cantors choristers dungcarts cartoonists driverless ubers penitent campers speeding cameras the bishop of Stockport hare krishnas Lutheran printers seal clubbers hanseatics bootlicks slapsticks nightsticks idolatrous selfie-takers improvident insurance vendors godless salts tars

stargazers hucksters lollards hookers hypocrites

The beadle drops to one knee beside Meg. His eyes close and his hands steeple. More mores without pause.

—buskers prophets curfew breakers dowsers divorcees Joan late of Kent persons of interest personnel carriers Benjamin Zephaniah nuns duns optic doctors the holy spirit the arch bishoprick dawdlers dying dead mudlarks many monkys dippers rough sleepers sidecar taxis tax avoiders taxiderms hullaboos deliveroos puffs and patties and fops!

The jaw, jawing, churns. The husk revolves. One socket scoops soil that it slings with the other. The shell claws from its rut, falls on its occipit, shouts.

—Transpontine privy acquaductal sewer of the shitty!

Lady Meg sighs. She gathers up the nog. Hush now, rest, she says. She puts pa on the wadding.

—I paid the axe that had struck him.

—That's no authority.

—It's a traitor's bonce off London Bridge!

—He should be feeding fish.

—Scant fare I'd be in cold Thames soup!

—My father. The ransom paid.

—His name, for the clerk.

—Sir Thomas More, Lord Chancellor, friend and adviser to the King.

As was, says the skull from its pillow, my fame's behind me he retired me.

The pale clerk returns.

—This nut's No More, the Pope Firster? Sir I mind him riding here.

By a cardinal red such rosing I'd not seen before.

His complexion is fair sings a voice way back in the dark. Who's there, calls the beadle. Windblown whispers drift through the way.

his face being

rather blonde than pale

with no approach to redness

except a delicate flush

which lights up the whole.

No way the skull objects no way I always looked like this.

The scowl by which we knew you's gone, shouts
As from the door. Who's thair the beadle calls, be
off he shouts, nothing here to see be off.

The red cardy was Wolsey, the skull blabs the clerk,
I remember our jolly to Rome. Bound to fail of
course he adds then on it clacks how young it once
was, how it wore a hair shirt the usual guff. By then
I've had enough. I swing our shutters wide. I turn
on all the lights. I dawn the tudor night.

—He profaned many such holidays!

They look up—beadle, clerk, lady, skull—their shadows sharp in electric light. With hands they shield
their eyes, all but the skull.

–That man's no angel, More's no saint!

The whispers rally, pushing back.

his countenance answers to his character

having an expression of

kind and friendly cheerfulness

a little air of raillereeeeee

Tell it to families of men he did roast, I snap back.

—Tell Tewkesbury, hote fyrebrande burnyng
at hys bakke that all the water in the worlde
wyll never quenche!

It weren't the church burned Took, bawls Meg.

—Was state!

—He set Bainham, Bayfield, Bilney, Dusgate,
Hitton blazing!

A King's servant but God's first, she screeches,
pointing to the vacant witbox, that's my father!

Love you loads babe drawls the skull. It pouts a lip-
less air kiss. The beadle approaches our door.

—A convicted traitor to the crown. Snuff that
lamp!

I comply. He's getting impatient. So's the Lady.
Their voices persist in the murk.

Give a girl a break she gasps.

—What more must I forfeit?

—You hint at a settlement? For treasonous
conveying! There's no permit for perfidy.
You hold no parchment for these remains.

There's precedent, heckles the skull, 'sbeen done
before.

—We gave the head of Buckingham back.

—Do you oppose the King?

I do not, says the Lady.

'Enery's an eretic rattles the skull.

—I'm no fan the crown can't hurt me now.

—Hold your tongue!

—Shame on you!

—What? Oh sorry, my bad! Cease I mean zip
it button your lip you know what I mean.

Fat prat Henry can't get it up, toots the skull, wilt
dick Henny's a traitor to the faith!

There's scuffling as two bodies tussle, the Beadle
and Lady I think.

—He did not go so far as buffooncry!

—Restrain him.

—How, if he will not?

—This bone is a relic for papist worship!

—I swear it will not be.

—You intend to lodge this corruption in
church?

—I will not. He'll bide at the house.

—Damn your pickles and preserves!

The scuffling ends.

—See to the clerk for the distress you cause.
Twenty shillings twice over.

She pays, she departs. He curses.

—Rome's bitch. More's bonemeal for Dunstan swine.

The beadle rides back to the city, the torch of the
clerk his star. I kindle my candle crown. I step
out. The ground beneath my feet obscures and
gleams, a furrowed blanket. I hurry to the spot
where the wagon stood.

Neighbours unbar their doors and gaggle at corners.
Gossip seeds rumour, birthing myth. More's not
dead. A witch in her finery. Beadle spellbound.
Spirits and conjury. The toothtug mouthing off.

The clerk had taken three steps with the basket. He
placed the cranium left. I rake cold gums of earth,
delving with my fingers. Pebbles glint. I search
the street's sour breath. A voice calls, Asis calling,
far off. What d'you seek? Leave well alone come in
let be. In grit a cream spot, I find it. A dislodged
tooth of Thomas More, saint to be. I raise it to my
crown. A molar incisor, much mineralised, with
mild attrition.

A prize piece in my collection.

M.J. Gilbert

Subverbs of Hell

"As I was walking among the fires of Hell . . .
I collected some of their proverbs . . .
the sayings used in a nation
mark its character . . ."

—William Blake, *Proverbs of Hell*

While traveling through a quiet village, I stopped to admire the quaint phrases on its welcome mats, bumper stickers, and living room walls. But when night fell, devils appeared and overturned the mats, peeled the stickers, and flipped the homely frames. There, on those opposing sides and inner surfaces, I read infernal musings. So I wandered the wastes of night and copied down the shadowy phrases. For I believe the secret proverbs of a village reveal its hidden character.

Those whose gardens eat their lawns have conquered a whole universe.

If the backyard were righteous, it would become the park.

The hum of the streetlight bids all good children home.

The solitary cat, eyes. The loyal dog, obedience.

The hours of acrimony are recounted in minutes. The minutes of acrimony are recounted for hours.

Only in the village can the perfection of cities finally be imagined.

The finished basement is the glory of winter.

The fly, exchange. The spider, use.

The supermarket, a borrowed cart; but every driveway, a car.

Whatever is impolitic, remove it to a sign and keep it by the road.

The fool watering a walled garden will never behold heaven nursing immeasurable fields of wildflowers.

The commuter train is a cavern, but earbuds are a hermitage.

After moving to the country, the dog receives the same leash while the cat receives a new kingdom.

The driveway of desire leads to the garage of plenty.

The road of stern responsibility runs beside the sidewalks of dizzy joy.

The streetlight, a mother's voice. The floodlight, a mother's eyes. The nightlight, a mother's song.

Rights are mapped in measured miles. Freedom is measured in acres.

Because the welcome mat cannot stand, it lies.

Where sprinklers are not, nature is.

The garden, creativity. Imagination, the oak.

The wisdom of elders and the laughter of children are the wages of harmony.

The pantry for wines that keep. The garden for trees that weep.

Put out the garbage on even days, signs on even years.

Hear the roar of the leaf blower, for it everywhere decrees a pure backyard.

The monarchs whose marriage beds are in high towers will fall to slumber beside low basins, but peasants in their ranches shall never be removed.

The clean street, the quiet neighbor, and the calm classroom are of worth beyond reckoning.

Nature blesses her weeds with the sweetest perfumes so the innocent will call them flowers.

What can never be too big shall always be too small.

Pennies for composing the manuscript of genius; a fortune for signing the paperwork of refinance.

After forty-five weeks comes the triumph of fresh tomatoes.

Ride in the morning. Drive at the noon. Idle in the evening. Park in the night.

Let the coastlines of the wealthy and the sidewalks of the poor be exchanged so the villages of workers may believe they've witnessed justice.

How pure is the world after garbage day.

The contentment of the goldfish will never be known by the carp.

The desert, the ocean, and the mountain range include without reservation.

The home calls its hearth sacred—the yard, its edges.

The open house shall welcome all but closes for the few.

Like esteemed friends, the best recycling bins are modest and discrete.

The coldest mountains make their home in the sky.

Main Street, Church Street, Bank Street, First Street. The most vital arteries carry the most precious blood.

Let the composted tomato seed bear fruit in the flower beds—it is a mighty dividend.

Pass on wealth so it may be grown.

Pass on property so it may be held.

Pass on what mustn't be said so it may remain silent.

The carp would have its grandeur if ambition were evenly rewarded.

Let it be said of memory that the road is of earth, the city of water, the town of air, the wilds of fire.

Shovel your snow far into the street—the plow is pitiless as the storm.

The body for labor. The mind for work. The soul for vocation.

New neighbors are closer than friends or enemies.

The village elder knows: what we intend is never as powerful as what we allow.

The busy Hummingbird knows neither work nor poverty.

If the Ants of ambition would take only what they need, they could recline with the Grasshoppers of plenty.

The priest, weeks. The doctor, years. The banker, decades.

The value of location is penury beside a wealth of space.

The city looks out on a dull, green waste.

The village sees only the heights of the city.

If the lawn shall drink our water and yield no fruit, let the cunning keep our money and make us glad.

Well-kept grass is trampled where wild tree limbs reclaim the sidewalk.

A generation for rights—for freedom, a lifetime.

The noisy labor of spring longs for the windy silence of winter.

The heart is always in a country home.

The city teaches. The village knows.

Those who have traveled by city and suburb say Heaven must dwell in the sky.

A prince's lot for foundling pups, but measured gruel for infants.

A few bare necessities is all one needs to become poor.

Where there are crumbs there are ants. Where there are shrubs there are deer. Where there are rooms there are children.

Like desire, the perfect closet receives but never fills.

Nature squirms whenever walled, but bows to fences well-installed.

The beauty of flesh leads the eye to sin, but a mortgage leads the soul to ruin.

Love your country. Betray your empire.

JOHN OLIVER HODGES

CORNICE WILD WITH TONGUE

One day Cornice took a picture of his tongue. This made Cornice want to take another picture of his tongue, so that's what Cornice did. By the time Cornice returned from his walk up the trail, he had taken more than 30 pictures of his freaking tongue. Over the next week, then into the following month, Cornice continued taking pictures of his tongue.

It was a thing. Instead of taking regular pictures, selfies that might actually serve a purpose, normal pictures that might be shared in the way of *Oh, look at me doing fun things out in nature*, no, Cornice clicked along on his idiot's tongue. Every time he clicked one off, like out in the woods alone, or up in the alpine, by rivers or whatever, he always stuck out that silly tongue.

Why? Why? What was it about? Why did Cornice do that? He just did it, never really stopping to ask why. *Stick out your tongue! Stick out your tongue!* He had a camera, so *stick out your tongue!*

The camera was digital, his first. His wife's mother gave it to Cornice as a going-away present while he and Chelsea yet lived in Florida, before they flew on over to Alaska. Though the camera sported too many controls to keep track of, it was pretty cool. You could take as many pictures as you wanted—*clickety clickety click*—and you didn't have to go to Walgreens or Eckerd Drugs to turn in the film for processing, which could be iffy if the rolls sported pictures of naked girls. Sure, Cornice had been there done that. Before picking his pictures up, he'd always got a little nervous in that his girlfriends looked young. What if the cops were there, waiting at Eckerd to put Cornice in cuffs?

It was crazy, wasn't it? A camera that kept on clicking? Wow. And here after Cornice had spent so much dumb time doing *real* photography, the whole black and white thing where you develop your own dumb film and buy light sensitive paper and put your dumb fingers in chemicals and wash your prints and make them archival, turning your stupid-ass pictures into bona fide masterpieces.

None of that was relevant anymore, so click away, bitch!

From the point of view of somebody normal it would've been weird, this thing Cornice kept doing that didn't make any sense at all, clicking off pictures of his tongue. It was not of his tongue only, of course. It was of himself sticking out his tongue. That meant his mouth was open and it was like he was licking the air, tasting nature, or maybe Cornice had his tongue out in the air in case a person walked by. Wouldn't that person, seeing Cornice with his tongue hanging out like a flag flapping around in the wind be like *Hey, maybe I should put my tongue against that guy's tongue*

and then we can be kissing, because everybody wants to kiss and be kissed, don't they? Everybody wants to love and be loved, don't they? In that, Cornice was like everybody else on the planet. In that, Cornice was your regular old everyday kind of dipshit.

It also happened, come to think of it, that when guys walked around alone in the woods, sometimes taking all their clothes off in that nobody else was around, only porcupines and bears and eagles and whatnot, their minds wandered into dreams that sometimes took on erotic edges. Could anybody deny it? A guy might think of, say, times from the past when the love was better than average, when the love was all-consuming and kept a fire burning in the heart.

Though Cornice's wife sometimes long-walked with him, even mountain-climbed up into the alpine while holding his hand, and though Chelsea also now and then took all her clothes off so Cornice could photograph her being one with nature, she all wrapped up in her insanely hot body, mostly it was Cornice out there, little ole Cornice all by his lonesome self.

Being alone had its charms. While alone you melded with nature better. The lack of distractions did that, and the air always was crazy fresh, the colors untouched and pristine, the sounds of water not even calming because you already were calm. The sounds were a part of you, and you were of them, the colors too were you, and the sky, the cries you heard from birds, the sights of deer flying through green valleys, it all ran in your veins while alone. In this place of peace you saw yourself unseparated from the world. You were the world. The world was you.

Or maybe the sticking out of his tongue that Cornice kept on doing for no good reason at all was provoked by a thing way deep down in the inside caverns of his self, a thing Cornice had no clue over, a thing that said what Cornice really wanted was a cock in his mouth.

Was it even possible? Is that why Cornice clicked off shots of himself with his tongue out? That he was in the closet? Oh, good Lord, highly unlily!

Jesus.

It wasn't like Cornice couldn't entertain the idea without getting nervous. It wasn't like Cornice could not imagine what it would be like. Cornice even guessed he could try it out for the hell of it if some friend or something, or maybe some stranger, said it would make him happy. Didn't Cornice like to see others happy? Hell yes he did! Granted, some things Cornice might never know about himself, but being gay, no, Cornice was pretty sure about that one. Nah, it didn't seem to be the case, and anyway it was a stupid thought to think in the first place. The only reason Cornice would've thought it was for the reason that everybody ever since he could remember had always been so up in arms about were you or were you not gay? Who cared?

What Cornice did know for sure about himself, as embarrassing as it was to admit, was he loved the way women looked, especially women not

all that beefed out in the flesh department, which was a thing pretty common nowadays no matter where you looked in the United States—there were just plumped-up people everywhere, both women and men, and Cornice loved plumped-up people too, for sure, no doubt about it even for a second, just for some reason he did not want to stick his tongue into their pussies. Maybe that was sad. Cornice felt like a real sonofabitch over it, but what could Cornice do about the things that Cornice knew about himself? It wasn't like Cornice had control over where he wanted to stick his tongue? In any event, if it would make whatever person happy, Cornice was more than willing to loan out his tongue, no matter what size or shape you came in. *Just tell me where you want me to put it, and I will put it there and do whatever you say with as much finesse and expertise as I can muster.* Cornice had always liked being useful. Cornice liked how he felt when people appreciated what he did for them.

Cornice also knew that despite his need to give and receive love, he was odd, different from others. Most people, as far as Cornice could see, all they ever thought of really, besides sex, was making loads of money so they could live comfortably, do fun things like ride bikes along the coast of New Zealand, or show themselves off. *Look at me in my sporty car, check out my house.* Cornice cared nothing for all that. Cornice hated it, simply despised the notion of doing stuff to justify his idiotic life.

He liked veggies, Cornice, liked working in the dirt. He liked making art. Cornice made enough money to pay his half of the rent, and buy beer at the Alaska Hotel and Bar now and then. That's all money was good for. Of course, it would have been super nice if the art Cornice made could pay the rent other than the other stuff Cornice always ended up having to do to make ends meet.

Though Cornice knew he'd never get paid for sticking out his idiotic tongue, that whether he took ten pictures of his tongue or ten thousand pictures of his tongue, he still wouldn't get paid for it, there was a time when he felt more hopeful over getting paid for taking great pictures, not of his tongue, but of people, and for making paintings and writing stories. There was even a time when art professors gave Cornice little somethings, a hundred bucks, say, to talk to their students about making great photos. At one event, Cornice put on a slide show. One of the photos to come up on the screen in front of the 60 students in the auditorium, was of his wife Chelsea, all naked and glowing on the heart pine floorboards of the shack where they lived at the time. It was one of the color photos that Cornice had stressed over when picking his negatives and prints up from Eckerd Drugs. After his presentation and responses to the students' ques-

tions, a girl came up to Cornice and said that she was the naked girl's cousin. It was an awkward moment there at the art department, but if Cornice was to be honest with himself, which he always was, he would not have minded putting his tongue into the cousin's body as well. Simply put, pretty was a thing not to be denied. Pretty was irresistible. Pretty put the idea of love to the test. If you were willing to stick your tongue into just any old woman's pussy, or suck on some guy's cock just because it would make him happy, what did that mean in terms of the woman you supposedly were in love with? Well, Cornice didn't know for sure, but he carried a guilt trip around with him wherever he went. Cornice did not know why life was like life was. Life was just life. Mostly the mysteries of life caused wonder, but sometimes, it was true, Cornice felt stressed when pondering his place in the world.

Maybe that's why Cornice walked around in the forest so much. Out there in the loneliness he found peace. Knowing that he had a cool wife to come home to kept Cornice steady and sane throughout his woodsy sojourns. Ideally, she would've been with him, but she wasn't into all the stuff he was into, what could Cornice do about that? She liked gourmet pizzas, things made of leather, objects that sparkled. Nothing wrong there. People were allowed to like what people wanted to like. Cornice liked that Chelsea liked stuff different from the stuff he liked.

What Cornice did not know about himself was that he, Cornice, was not all there, that he, Cornice, was and had been mentally unstable since forever. He was and had always been overly emotional. He was a freak, had an enlarged amygdala, and Chelsea was right when complaining of his insensitivity to the feelings of others, say-

ing, "You can't see yourself!"

Didn't Cornice depend too much on Chelsea? He did, and was a crybaby, a potential suicide, was bad with rejection, and since when did anybody get to skate through life without being subject to rejection and ill-will and malevolent intentions? Grow up, asshole. It's a part of the program. Cornice was a bad accident waiting to happen, a "piece of work," as Chelsea also sometimes claimed.

Eventually Cornice tired of sticking his dumb tongue out, and of clicking off pictures of his dumb tongue getting stuck out for no apparent reason other than that he might be wanting to suck on a big fat cock. Frustrated, Cornice decided to mix things up a little, so took a tripod with him into the wilderness, where he took off his clothes. He attached the camera to the tripod and set the timer for ten seconds. That gave Cornice plenty of time to arrange himself in some interesting way that might make a neat picture. Once the shot had been made, Cornice went and looked at it on the digital camera screen, thought it was pretty neat, so took another, and another and another. Because he had taken a few pictures of himself naked now, he had to continue to take pictures of himself naked. It was that whole thing again about how if you stuck out your tongue once and took a picture, you had to keep on sticking out your tongue and taking more pictures. In his mind, Cornice likened it to trying to swim from Florida to Africa. After getting a little tired would he chicken out and swim back in the direction of Florida, or keep swimming in the direction of Africa, even while knowing he might drown trying to get there? That's what things were like for Cornice. Whenever he started something, he had to keep on going on that thing, just a-going and a-going.

Now, when Cornice entered the wild, he always took off all his clothes. Cornice clicked off tons of himself naked. Why not? With digital, the roll never ran out. Cornice did himself on hands and knees in leaves, hugging trees, walking paths, leaning over puddles in muskeg as the sun rose, and chasing after deer. He did himself in the alpine, half submerged in icy water, looking out over the city below in the pose of Christina from the Edward Hopper painting. Corniced clicked off shots of himself balancing precariously on cliffs and weird rocks. There's Cornice squatting at the opening of a little cave,

some kind of gnomic creature guarding a treasure. There's Cornice on his back in the mud, looking dead, arms drawn back as though just released from a torture rack. Some of the shots, the nudies—call it like it is—were quite good. Some looked like they belonged in museums, blown up for the eyes of art lovers and tourists, but Cornice knew they would end up in his newly expanding archive of jpeg files, never to see the light of day. Shit made him feel like a real fucking idiot, a real freako, a moron, but he did it anyway, continued walking in the woods and clicking off those pointless-ass pictures of himself, the lonely sensation deepening, drawing him into trances where he felt a kind of gargantuan void around him, a thing he could not see, only sense in the abstract. Though Cornice could not touch this thing with his fingers, it announced itself as real, a force dark yet bristlingly alive, it existed in tandem with the brightness of the real world that surrounded him visibly. At first it had been disconcerting, sensing the invisible force. It had crept up on Cornice, taking him unawares, as they say in the bible, but Cornice got used to it, and when entering the forest did not resist when it accosted him, enshrouding him. Cornice could tell that it was endless, that if you were to somehow step out of this world and into that one, it would not matter how far out you swam. You could swim all day, all month, all year, your whole lifetime and still never see the shore on the other side. The invisible force did not comfort Cornice. It really just made him feel more alone, more lonely and wishing he could somehow be all the people of the world at the same time.

One day, upon returning from his nature excursion, Cornice told Chelsea about how he'd been taking nude photos of himself out in the forest. She said, "Cool, let me see," so Cornice downloaded the pictures onto his computer and

Chelsea sat with him at the table, drinking a vodka tonic, and they looked at the pictures together, Cornice advancing them one by one with the mouse. "My God, these are beautiful," Chelsea said. "Why have you been keeping these from me?"

"I don't know. It's weird."

"That never stopped you before."

"Can I get a sip of that?"

"Sure." Chelsea handed her drink to Cornice. "You want one?"

Cornice took a sip and said, "That'd be great, I'd love one."

Chelsea whipped up a drink for Cornice and then there they were again, sitting side by side at the round kitchen table upon which the used desktop computer screen featured naked pictures of Cornice. It was kinda weird looking at naked pictures of himself with somebody else right beside him. "Holy cow," Chelsea said in response to the picture where Cornice was on his hands and knees, the balls there and you could see the sphincters. Chelsea licked her lips and shook her head. "If I was a gay guy and saw this I would be totally floored. I think I'd be careful who you show this to, baby."

"Wait, what? Show this to? How could I ever show these to anybody but you?"

"I don't know. I'd say they qualify as art, but some of this is super erotic. If I was a guy I'd totally wanna fuck that."

"No way."

"Yes way, ha ha."

"I had no idea," Cornice said.

Chelsea laughed on. Cornice felt happy hearing her happy. He wanted to hug her straightaway, but also wanted her to see the rest of the pictures because he had already showed her a bunch and now he simply had to show her all of them. He clicked the mouse. More pictures came up. Chelsea oohed and ahhed, Cornice feeling special and fortunate to know her. Looking at Chelle's shiny awestruck face, Cornice felt overcome with appreciation, and he said, "I love you, Chelle."

"Hey, I love you too, you know that."

"Yes, I know," Cornice said, "but lately, I don't know . . ."

"Lately? Lately? Lately what?"

"I don't know, I've just been feeling this weird sensation whenever I go back in the woods. Something comes over me. I feel like it's all about to end. I don't want it to end. I want it to go on forever. I want to keep on being me but if I can't be me I'll be perfectly happy if I can be somebody else, but I can't be somebody else. Life isn't like that, I know, I don't know, Chelle, I think I'm afraid. I wish I could stop it but deep inside I sense that I'm really afraid. It comes out of nowhere. It hits me and I feel so insecure. I probably have nothing to worry about, I just—"

"Hey," Chelsea said. She set her drink down and sort of wrapped her arms around Cornice. She pulled him her way so that Cornice slipped off his chair onto his knees, his head now in her lap. She put her fingers in his hair, comforting him.

"I'm afraid," Cornice admitted, and began crying.

"Hey now," she said, and said, "Let's get on the futon," so they did that, and then Cornice was just hugging her so tight, thinking he would never let her go. He really wanted to stay like this forever, just hug her and cry into her chest, into her heart. The tears soaked her shirt and Cornice rubbed his head around like he was a rodent or something without hands to help him along in life, only a mouth, which he used against her buttons until her shirt came free and then everything was all so natural. He was like a baby now, her amazing pale breast in his mouth and Cornice felt swept away in the abstractions of that other world, the chaos that he kept feeling whenever he went into the woods, the thing that was close enough to touch, yet always out of reach. It folded around him as the spittle on her nipple took on that smell, a smell of self and togetherness, a damp love that Cornice had always found compelling. Cornice moved his rodent's head back and forth across her chest like Stevie Wonder at the piano, how Stevie swung his head side to side flowingly in his blindness, both of her nipples flipping across Cornice's nostrils and eyes and then Cornice latching onto one and sucking, wholly satiated, even though no milk came out, and without a care in the world. For now, he was home.

REYoung

Dreaming of Water in a Season of Drought

The first thing he became aware of was the terrible thirst. His lips felt dry and cracked, his tongue swollen, his mouth and throat as desiccated as the burning desert. He also couldn't open his eyes. Maybe he was sick. Maybe he was dying. He pictured himself lying in a hospital bed, IV tubes, urine-soaked sheets. More than anything he desired a glass of water.

When at last he was able to open his eyes he found himself lying next to a large wooden barrel. Even odder, when he tried to move, he discovered he couldn't. To make matters worse, he lay in such a way that he couldn't see his body or any of his appendages. Had he had an accident? Fallen and broken his neck?

A faint gleam drew his eye to a single drop of water clinging to one of the barrel staves, inches from his face. Suddenly his terrible thirst returned and he yearned for the drop of water as if it were life itself. With a tremendous effort he stretched his head forward and, grimacing like a Maori warrior, caught this aqueous pearl on the very tip of his tongue. It was like drinking a diamond. It tasted the way he imagined heaven would taste. A wave of clear, cold water bathed his entire being. The sensation disappeared, his thirst grew even greater.

He stared at the spot where the drop of water had appeared. He desired another drop with the fervor of a religious convert. Slowly, miraculously, by an impossible process of osmosis through which the water seemed to be extruded from the barrel by his willpower alone, another drop oozed out of the rough wooden stave. Again, with a great effort, he was able to capture the drop on his tongue. Again the pure liquid flooded his entire being.

He repeated this process again and again. Each time he concentrated on that spot. Each time, after the same interval, another drop of water appeared. Each time, with the same effort, he caught it on his tongue.

Finally, after what seemed like hours of this torture, he regained enough strength to survey his surroundings. He seemed to be lying on the dirt floor of a small, dimly lit room with mud-brick walls. It was completely empty except for the barrel. Beyond that he could determine nothing else. He had no idea how long he'd been here in this condition. In fact, he had no memory of anything.

He closed his eyes. Maybe if he tried to focus on a particular event it might trigger a cascade of memories he could peel apart like the pages of a waterlogged book until he arrived at this moment. He concentrated. Nothing came to mind. He rebuked himself and tried harder. Still nothing. Not a person's face. Not a place or location. Not a job or avocation. Nothing.

He had a brief lucid thought. Was it madness? Had he lost his mind? Was he lying in an insane asylum, strait-jacketed, in a drugged stupor, all this his imagination?

Or what if he had had a terrible accident? What if he was not only paralyzed but amnesiac?

Panic-stricken, he struggled to free his uncertain limbs from uncertain shackles. To no avail. The effort exhausted him. He decided to rest for now. Maybe he would eventually recover enough strength to move. As long as one precious drop of water appeared after another.

Rather than comfort him, this thought brought him suddenly awake again. Until this moment he had imagined that he would go on sipping these vital drops of water forever, that the barrel was brimming over with cool, sweet water, fed, perhaps, by a hidden mountain spring. But now he began to fear that the barrel might be nearly empty, that what little water remained would soon be gone.

He must have finally fallen asleep. He woke to discover that a boy and girl had entered the room. Oddly, rather than calling out to them for help, he felt terrified. He tried to shrink back into the shadows and make himself as small as possible. Even more oddly, the boy and girl didn't seem to see him. They were both beautiful children, he noticed now. The boy had dark, flashing eyes, a strong jaw and high cheekbones.

The girl's eyes were a brilliant green. Lustrous black curls fell around her face.

Then he saw that they both had metal pails. They had come for water—*his* water. But they were so careless. As they dipped their pails into the barrel, they laughed and splashed water on each other. He wanted to cry out, *Stop! You're wasting my precious water!*

Suddenly he became aware of the girl's breasts heaving against her wet dress. How had he been so mistaken? They weren't children at all, but a young man and young woman. Now they began to undress while they continued to splash each other with water. The pure, vital liquid flowed between the young woman's naked breasts, down over her smooth belly and between her thighs. Clear, clean water splashed over the young man's lean, muscular chest and his erection springing up like a healthy young sapling.

Embracing awkwardly, as if this were their first time together, the couple dropped to the dirt floor and began to make love. Only now, as if in a dream, he had taken the young man's place. Rapturously, with complete abandonment, he kissed the girl's lips, her throat, her breasts. Greedily he drank up the small pool of water collected in her navel, lapped at the damp spring between her thighs. It was as if the girl herself had become water and he couldn't drink enough. He swallowed great mouthfuls of the cold, sweet water. But—something was wrong. Now the water tasted salty and bitter like urine. Wet sand filled his mouth. Coughing and sputtering, he spat it out.

When he opened his eyes again, the young man and woman were gone. He remembered the water they had spilled and felt a crushing despair. He stared at the spot on the wooden stave and waited.

The next time he woke it was dark, cold, night. Powdery white moonlight slanted through the narrow doorway, which he had only now noticed. Suddenly he felt afraid. What if a wolf or a lion entered and ravaged his helpless body?

The moonlight disappeared and the black rectangle of the doorway filled with stars. If he knew more about the science of astronomy, he might venture a guess as to his location.

The following morning there was another surprise. A woman entered, carrying a pail and a small bundle of laundry. She looked tired, her face worn and gray. And yet, she had obviously been pretty once. She shuffled across the room to the barrel, bent over it and, with some difficulty, filled her pail. Then she began to wash the laundry which, he saw now, was nothing more than rags. And yet she worked diligently, scrubbing and scrubbing. But even after she had used all the water in the pail, the rags still came out gray.

A man entered. He must have been handsome once, with a strong jaw, high cheekbones and flashing black eyes. Now he looked brutish, heavy. His face was worn and contorted with anger. Shaking the dripping rags in the woman's face, he yelled, "These clothes aren't clean!"

"But there isn't enough water," the woman said, looking terrified.

"Don't lie to me!" the man shouted. He glanced about and demanded, "Where are the children?!"

The woman looked even more terrified. "What children?"

"The children you promised me!" the man shouted. "I've wasted my entire life with you! And what have I gotten in return? Nothing!" And raising his hand, he slapped her across the face.

The woman began to cry, deep, gasping sobs.

She seemed so miserable, so wretched. What had brought her to this state? A great sadness came over him and he too began to weep. Hot, salty tears streamed down his face and into his mouth.

Then he was alone again. The barrel stood in front of him. He waited for a drop of water to appear. His thirst was greater than it had ever been. But still no drop appeared.

He decided he must be dying. Oddly, he felt philosophical about this prospect. It was simply another process. The evaporation of the self. Eventually he would cease to exist altogether. There would be nothing left to mourn, not a body, nor anyone to mourn that body. At least it would be better than the paralysis of this barren existence.

He heard a loud boom and something began to pound on the roof. He smelled dust. A cool mist blew in the door. It was raining.

Joe Taylor

Timeless Love

DESPITE WHAT one might think about soothing 3/4 waltz measure or tricky 6/8 that can masquerade as 2/4, musicians do not make kind lovers. This sad fact has been proven over all my experiences. Perhaps musicians reside solely in a perfectly happy sphere where notes and time signatures shape their bones and flesh and blood, neither allowing nor desiring any other intrusions.

Mozart obstinately remained in childhood—no doubt with encouraging help from his father. Beethoven's brow continually stormed, reflecting contemporary politics. Could either man reserve any time to soothe a mate? If so, it would be some troublesome signature such as 9/8.

Today's rock musicians? To further prove their dedication to themselves and their faithful public, they insist music must subsume their entire lives, and they employ the help of drugs or alcohol or both in at least outwardly guaranteeing this—with obvious, resultant detriment to their mattress performance. Even 9/8 moves out of range. From the one view I had of her, Janis Joplin led the women's crusade in accomplishing the same.

Poets? Just as music overtakes musicians, words and emotions overtake poets. *Ah! That vase (vahhzz) of dried flowers (flahhhrrzz)! It timelessly subsists as the perfect, shimmery (chhimmery) robin's egg blue! / Ah! Indeed, Fluffmouth! It's just too bad those flowers wilted two weeks back and now fall flaking to mar the table's lustrous finish. Much the same, I fear, as any mate would mar under your misplaced exuberances.*

Artists? With their fingers dipped in oils, smudging all that they touch? For real?

Actors? Film stars? Just where does truth lie with them? Are they not always rehearsing?

Sculptors? Oh dear, who wants to be bludgeoned abed?

Accountants? *Last time we lasted four minutes and fifteen seconds. Should we try for four minutes and nineteen?*

But lo! Consider bakers! Therewith, ladies, you will encounter competent, patient, attuned, mindful lovers, Sleepy Phillipe serving as my most vivid example.

Li-Li's hands stayed strong, huge, yet soft as a downy feather pillow and always moist from yeast and dough. At dusk, a mouse would skitter over cobblestones at our approach and Li-Li would unlock the back room of our bakery. Upon the instant the door undertook its creaking way to admit us, Li-Li would hum bass notes in a frivolous non-tune tune, and those notes would emerge from his swaying huge torso into the shop's surrounding air. They would float over every proofing shelf. They would ease across the central worktable. They would tumble into my ears and vibrate through my neckbones to engorge my breasts. In winter, Li-Li would amble like a gentle fairy tale giant to toss more logs onto our oven's glowing fire. In summer, he'd stir the embers and add kindling. As the oven heated, he would stroll to caress each bag of flour, each jar of honey or molasses, our single sack of leavening salt. And gradually, as he extended through the room, his bass would shift to a tenor. This shift always brought a moment where I would pause and smile, for Li-Li had picked up the lilting British tune

"Greensleeves" from sailors, and that song remained his favorite to sing through the workings of night. I would listen and watch as he'd bend his great, muscular rump to open our small cooling cellar where we stored the yeast, I would watch and listen as his discordant humming would transform into melodious lyrics, "A-las, my lo-ove, you do me wro-ong, to cast me ou-out discourteously." And he would lift and cradle the yeast to his enflamed breast.

When the yeast reached room temperature and the waiting water/honey or water/molasses mixture had warmed sufficiently, Li-Li would mix them, stirring carefully so as not to break the yeast's tiny, growing stems, then adding the smallest amount of leavening, crystalline salt. "Green-slee-eves was my de-li-ight, Greensleeves was all my joy." His head would tick-tock tilt as a glorious foam happily frothed to make itself known. His fingers could not help themselves: they would begin to twitch. In response, my pelvis would undertake its own twitch.

At last, succumbing to a type of miniature ballet, his fingers dipped into the flour, sprinkling it downward, slowly at first, then more rapidly as the mound revealed her readiness. At that instant, I would sigh and enjoin my hands with his. Together, together, together we sifted in the flour. Together, together, together we would watch it precipitate downward like a cool stream overflowing a rocky ledge.

Li-Li always composed the doughs in great three- or four-kilo balls, kneading each tenderly while singing. He claimed music coaxed the dough into rising as he folded and refolded and re-refolded her. I always agreed plenteously, often enough halting my own measuring or dividing to listen to his voice and sway in its dovelike coo. An occasional pat—pip!—and he would place his nose to the dough, inhaling deeply, as a lover might breathe the beloved's hair. Then, more gentle kneading. "Green-slee-eves is all my love, Green-sleeves is al-ll my heart."

He would stop at that chorus and bend to listen, as if he could hear the yeast and honey and flour respiring and yearning amidst the salt leavening. Perhaps he could. A baker's quirk of his was to run a furrow down the middle of each inhaling, pulsing mound. He claimed this added extra breathing area for the yeast and honey and flour to grow. He would ease the side of his palm, always his right one, along the mound until the cleft ran deeply enough to suit him. Or rather, to suit the dough. "Each dough reacts differently, Francine. I must give her whatever particular space and warmth she desires," he whispered on the very first night we worked together. Oh, it was eternal love for me! Then he placed his arm around my waist, and together we kneaded, we tugged, and we swayed.

When pleased with the cleft's intensity and depth, Li-Li would always give a last pat and move off—not far, just a few steps—to allow the dough privacy to pulse on her own, always softly singing so she would know she was not forgotten as he prepared another mound. On occasion, he would return, humming assurance: "I've not deserted you, my sweet." He would tenderly insert his thumb to measure elasticity. "Your moisture is nearly perfect," he'd coo. "And your temperature, ah, has turned divine." Twittering his fingers, he would blow her a kiss.

Such was the amazing attentiveness Li-Li gave each brooding mound of dough.

And then the moment would arrive to separate the great mound into loaves! Many a time I turned faint and warmly moist myself watching him coddle the elastic dough into five or six separate loaves. He would knead each loaf ever so softly, not wanting to compromise her inner growth, her readiness to expand, her desire to burgeon her way into the world. "And who but my la-a-dy Greensleeves?"

Then, placed on a bed in the oven, each loaf would soon enough blossom, turning as golden as the sun. Li-Li would tap a knuckle on her side to hear the returning, happy hollowness indicating that the loaf had given her all.

That is how a baker makes love . . .

W.J. Davies

The Man in the U-Bend

It's awful. The worst thing is I don't know what brought it on. Everything was fine. I could go five, six, even seven days without a break. I'd wake up full of ideas, full of energy, and away I'd go. Suddenly, the wall. It hit me square in the face. Or I hit it. Ever since, nothing.

I haven't plumbed anything for six months.

Six months of plumber's block. Six. Months.

Do you know what it does to you, being a plumber who can't plumb? Never mind the financial mess it's left me in. It's my identity. At dinner parties, out for drinks, around town, that's how I'd introduce myself. Hi there, what do you do? I'm a plumber, I'd say, and damn proud of it, I'd think. No one expects you to say *plumber*, and they look at you a little differently for the rest of the evening. Have you plumbed anywhere I know, they ask? What's the plumber so and so like? Would you sign this basin wrench?

Inevitably, there are always those people who tell you being a plumber is a tough career choice. It's difficult to get your first break. Hard to make a steady income. Mainly luck, not talent. Only celebrity plumbers make any real money now and they all have ghost plumbers behind them. You'll struggle against the corporatisation of the trade. I've heard it all.

I've wanted to be a plumber ever since I helped my brother unclog his sink at university. One night, he dropped acid and tried to stop demons invading his bathroom by filling the plughole with flour. I arrived the following morning to find him curled up on the floor, wrapped in the shower curtain for warmth. He looked like a corpse during a police investigation, though someone had written LIMP DICK PUSSY in marker pen on his forehead, which would be unusual for most murders. For some reason, the scene stirred in me the need to unclog the sink. I found some rubber gloves and got to work.

Twelve years later, I'm the most reputable plumber in the county. I've done it all, from a church's ancient sewage pipe to a cabinet minister's toilet clogged with evidence. I'm discreet, I'm neat. It's engineering meets installation art. What I do, it matters.

Then, all of sudden, the wall. It came when I was draining an elderly couple's radiator. They were having damp proofing done and needed the fixings removed. I was an integral part of the whole plan. But during the third of the six radiators, I drew a blank. I just sat and stared at the piping. My grip loosened on the valve as nothingness invaded my mind. A drip formed and before long black water washed over the living room floor. I was utterly bewildered. The couple were livid. As they screamed at me to fix it, to stop the horrible water soaking into their Persian rug, their German Shepherd came in and started lapping at the sludge. I think I entered a kind of daze, a fugue state, I've heard it called, and my whole personality drained away. Unblinking, unspeaking, I got up and left. Slowly, over the following days, I returned to myself, but whenever I tried to think about the plumbing job, I couldn't get past it. I could see it in my mind so clearly: halfway through the turn of the wrench, and I couldn't go on.

Some people say plumber's block isn't real. You can push through if you just get on with it. Treat plumbing like work, not art. Get into a routine. Use those golden hours in the morning to plumb before your mind is too aware of itself. Drink more coffee. Drink less coffee. Plumb drunk. Quit booze altogether. Plumb at night, after everyone else has gone to bed. Just show up and plumb.

You name it, I've tried it. It's all a load of shit. Every single time, there's the wall. I'm a shell of myself. I just sit around watching videos of plumbing.

I'm considering retraining, forging a new identity, getting some distance and maybe even earning some decent money again. Someone suggested I give writing a go. How hard can it be? It's just words on a page.

Chapter One

The Man in the U-Bend.

Yeah, that's good. Let's stick with that. Words on a page. How hard can it be?

Ian Boulton

Futureproofing Against Nominative Determinism

I t's likely, I'm thinking, that one morning I will wake up and you won't. There will be no warning. The previous night you will have turned away from me as usual and left me to my reading for another twenty minutes or so. I will have turned off my bedside light, unconcerned, and settled down to sleep. On waking, I will sit up and check for messages on my phone, maybe scan the headlines, letting you have a few more minutes' kip before we have to get on with the day. A short spell will pass before I venture a 'good morning' or a 'sleep well?' A small shake will follow, then something more robust. With the sense that something is wrong I will turn you over and the fact of your death will take shape, hitting me like the obvious. I will

I share my full name with one of the bad ones. One everybody recognises. The neighbours. The smell. The drains. The trophies kept in the fridge

need to do a couple of things immediately. The materials needed for my next steps are safely tucked away in my side of the wardrobe. There will be no need to check. In the meantime, carefully, respectfully, I will ease myself out of bed as if I am worried about your being disturbed. Granting you a dignity in death that I oftentimes forgot to afford you in life. Then, dressing gown on, I will leave the bedroom and make for the boiler on the landing. There I will

Luckily none of the atrocities happened . . . sorry, they were not discovered . . . until I had left school. Imagine that! Take any embarrassment I have experienced in my adult life and times that by a significant number

turn off the heating in the hallway, open the front door just enough so that a moderate breeze or firm knock will see it wide open. I imagine a neighbour, an Amazon delivery driver, a police officer coming in and calling up the stairs. Then make my way to the kitchen. I will drink a glass of water and perhaps wish there was a bottle of booze I could take a slug from. But I don't think I will

The day when the news first hits, it's over at long last, relief in the region, disgust at the fresh horrors, at last we know say some parents, how did this happen under the noses of the neighbours/family/police

require much in the way of Dutch courage to sit beside you, resting my back against our headboard, slip that hidden plastic bag that is the perfect size and strength over my head and fix it tight around my neck with my old school tie. But first I will

Then the horror that strikes very few of us. How many? A hundred or so, I believe. Our lives have to go on, changed forever. What innocents we had been till that morning

place the empty glass in the sink and I will walk along the hallway to our living room, check the radiator hasn't come on, unlock and open the long glass doors that lead on to our garden. These I will fling wide, letting the morning air fill the house. Will I look out at the grass, the bushes, our tree? No. In fact, I see myself carrying out all these tasks with eyes deliberately out of focus. I won't wish to take anything in. Anyway

Pretending to find it amusing, hearing every imaginable joke over and over again. Taking offense, giving offense, ignoring, getting in the first shot, putting it out there, puzzlement and feigned ignorance. Nothing helps

it's just as likely, I'm thinking, that I will enter a roundabout without paying due care. Perhaps I will have one of those peripheral visual hallucinations that have begun to plague me . . . a cat or a small dinosaur . . . You will be doing your usual, just jabbering away in the passenger seat about matters that are none of my concern, can never hold my interest. Or hang on a minute. Surely

The before and after. The plates shift, a mountain range rises cutting off my short past from my endless future

one day I will turn up for the results of some test or other and be dealt a piece of devastating news. I will be alone with the doctor, as is my custom. I have no time for those who say they need support on these occasions, have spent the past hour silently scoffing at them in the corridor outside the office. Handholding. Weeping, some of them. I will ask how long and receive the doom-laden answer phlegmatically. At that moment I will decide to refuse all treatment. Simultaneously, I will decide not to tell you. Especially as

People have never known what to say. Whether to ignore, whether to acknowledge, whether to make a small joke or empathise, feel my discomfort. Did I notice the double take? People, they worry. People, they can't wait to rush home and tell

it's more than likely, I'm thinking, that it's you that will be driving and I will be asleep in the passenger seat, a little worse for wear, and it's your mind that will wander because there is no stimulation coming from my direction. You need me to keep you engaged with the world around you. You've always been that way. Yes, there is no reason that I will be to blame. It will be all your fault. You will be daydreaming. You've never undertstood

The head in the fridge. Everybody fixates on the head in the fridge

but I will be pretty pleased with myself when I imagine responding to your enquiry about the results with a breezy, 'Nothing to report. Same old same old. Do less of this, do more of that.' You will be oblivious

From time to time I come across somebody similarly, but not exactly, afflicted. We exchange a look that says 'don't think you understand . . . my guy is worse than your guy because he is from this country/in that movie/more recent/more disgusting/still alive' . . . it's a complicated exchange

to my heroism, not realise that I am sparing your feelings, taking away all that anxiety, all that pain. Saving myself, too, from all that dreary talk. During the short time that follows my fatal diagnosis you will ask me to do many normal things. There will be nails and screws, pipes and wrenches, mowing and dusting, parcels to package and deliver to friends I will never see again. I hug these sweet thoughts tightly, keep them close. I realise that I could, if I wished to reveal my upcoming agony, cry off from the mundane. This is not how anybody would choose to spend their final days, is it? But I will be struck by my own bravery, decency and sacrifice to such a degree that I will carry out my little chores cheerfully. You may think something is going on as I have never behaved in this uncomplaining manner before. I will

I have considered contacting the others in the (exact) same position. To find out if my response is in, you know, proportion. I was going to say those nearest to me in age but, of course, there are no younger versions. No parent would

never stop blaming myself for letting you drive when I know how your mind wanders when I am not conscious enough to engage it. What kind of idiot does that? The same kind of idiot who lets me drink when we go out just so they can complain about it later. Well, thanks to you, this time there will be no later. I will

Sometimes I am unable to attend a work meeting and my absence is noted in the minutes. Apologies . . . Who isn't going to laugh at that? It was too late to change it. There was never any question: I was stuck with it. It was me as well as him

be worried, of course, about when to spill the beans, confess that I have been soldiering on bravely for these past two, three, four months but now the time has come when I can no longer disguise my discomfort, pain, weakness, need for consolation. The look you give me at this point will delight me. Your admiration, your gratitude, your warmth, will help to ease me to my ending, knowing that I did the right thing, that I showed my love and consideration for you in the depths of my dying. I will ponder the meaning of *in sickness and in health*, understanding it now as an internal message and not, as suspected, a prosaic duty of care. But, my God, it's better

It's the one area of life where time does not pass. It never goes away. No sooner has one generation faded and forgotten than another is brought to life by fucking Netflix

than the likelihood, I'm thinking, that we will miss the boat, me and you. Opportunities to make a choice for ourselves will come and go as we think, maybe next time . . . That's how we find ourselves side by side propped up on oversized plastic-backed beige armchairs in what looks to be a 1950s conservatory. Opposite us sit our mirror images, open-mouthed, closed eyes, a forgotten lowbrow magazine resting on their laps. There is a smell of mince in the air. High in the corner a hyperactive young cunt is yelling from the TV that we could win something or other. Nobody is watching him. Only one or two can even hear him. It is 10.30 in the morning and it feels as if the day will never end. I will

What could I have been if he hadn't got there before me? Because of his reality then any good I might have done has been diluted by who did it. Any bad has paled in comparison

slip into my old parka in the dead of night. Or what if

I'm on high alert.. The notorious photo can appear at any time and in any company. The office. The gym. The

dentist. Any excuse for them to wheel it out once more is a good excuse. The marriage of the survivor. The pool table, the satellite tv, the access to drugs, phones, the internet, his lover the guard tells all. The worst since. Fucking Netflix

it's me that has to accompany you to that chilly hospital corridor? It's me that has to hold your hand, sitting across the desk from a doctor that seems reluctant to look up from his notes. You get the bad news and I get to play the dutiful one, the selfless companion that does everything to ensure that your final days are filled with light and compassion. Not having to

I did consider adopting a jaunty nickname but it would never fly. My jauntiness died in those drains

make the walk down to the beach in the dark and cold, stand there stuffing pebbles into the parka's saddlebag pockets, wade out into the waves under the moon like some unhappy genius. And that will never happen because

Those shocking shop window moments. That stop me in my tracks. See the floppy schoolboy fringe and that slope to the shoulders as if this guy is trying to hide inside his own body. The glassiness in the eyes that was captured in that photo has become mine. I will shave my head and stand up a little straighter for a bit but soon the hair grows back, the posture crumbles. He seeps back in

it is more than likely, I think, that one day I will simply not be around. The open door will bring in a neighbour, that Amazon delivery driver, the police, a burglar. They will enter the silent house, walk down the empty hall, call out is anybody here, feel its chill, choke on the clouds of sickly sweet air freshener. They will see a desolate living room and beyond that a garden that seems forlorn, blighted. Is blighted. They will back up and enter the kitchen and see the yellow post-note on the fridge that reads DO NOT OPEN

Bradley David Waters

Bore Report Part Fore

Some mornings so ordinary
I could plant a feather tree
in my corner of the arc
in the ring. Strangle its

Victorian whisps & vapors
with lemon meringue & mood
stabilizers. This is not
conjecture or obfuscation.

This work is loaded & careful;
stacked like an old Swede would do.
When no more can be afforded,
stick a dream seed in its goop.

Some mornings so frosted &
festooned I sprout clinical
admonishments & dancehalls
of '82 buttercream carnations.

By clock watch & gobble hour,
bluebirds bring a powder blue tux.
Fresh off the uncle who OD'd
on Percocet on a brick bunk;

unencumbered by a quiet
brother in Denver or a
DJ playing Juice Newton.
The rest is sulfur spray for

the royal cherry. The ruddy
mildew cocktail plop of last-
ditch efforts. Penny eyes for
penny ideas—and I'm on top.

I'm fizzing with early burps
of clonazepam and that
other gentle nudger that sorta
staples my brow with feathers.

No uncles or aunts left; not
until they die anyway. Then,
watch for Victoria's blowhole.
Thar she blows her limoncello!

Carl Landauer

She had been registered for Vassar at birth

Sidney Lumet's The Group (1966)
after Mary McCarthy's The Group (1963)

There in the very first sentence
    Kay Leiland Strong, Vassar '33
as McCarthy's voice
in alumnae newsletter chattiness
cleaves to the group voice.
Lumet in his turn will turn
to gossipy lunches and phone calls
and Helena's newsletter typing words
across the screen
    letter by letter
ending in exclamation points
    On to bigger things, Priss!
We almost forget
there's a Depression going on,
sure, there are occasional references
and money challenges,
but Lumet's credit sequence
starting with saddle shoes
in military or dance precision
suggests a vague time just past,
not Depression's depth.

Despite their obvious obliviousness,
their cattiness,
we're drawn mainly to their
own tragedies,
the fine white Renaissance nostril
was dinted with a mark of pain.
To the men who are horrors—
Kay's philandering, alcoholic failed playwright,
Priss's overbearing pediatrician husband
pushing breast-feeding beyond exhaustion
Libby's near rape,
Kay's husband committing her,
institutionalizing her in rage,
a page, it turns out,
from McCarthy's own life.

But it's not a matter of finding
the key to some roman à clef
but laughing at McCarthy's
layers of inside jokes.
There among the few books
on a shelf is *Axel's Castle*,
the famous book by her husband.
And for Kay's funeral,
Lakey knows just where to go,
     straight off to Fortuny's
to buy her
     an off-white silk pleated gown—
the kind the Duchess of Guermantes used to receive in
and we know that Mary
expects us to know
the fuss Proust made
of the Duchess and Fortuny,
but now, decades later,
we must be missing
untold bottled messages.

GRAHAM CLIFFORD

GIFT TOKENS

I'm helping squirrels communicate with horses. I'm a geranium. This is not a drill. A pink sun has risen fizzy with hornet larva. They are eating it from inside. You can see them jerk and flex in preparation.

We drink radiator water. Someone hopeful was gashed and bled out so quickly. Completely empty, but with time to dispassionately contemplate a foil number-balloon escaping into cumulus.

I will employ a sociopath to join our team in case we need to shoot someone in the back of the head to make corned beef rations last. The blueprint of our office's air ducts is also the map of how to get to your heart.

Elegiac, Amnesiac, Insomniac, Heart Attack

A New Jersey Percival in media res without seeing the *res* for what they are;
Were they better seen for what they were not—look that way from afar?

Pale Horse, Hot Dog (*Hot-Dog* in French), Curse, Beach, Frog, Lovers, Fool, Empress;
Did you select from this deck to choose the cold Grail you sought to impress?

A decorative friend, good to have here in the long summer prologue;
Did the world read a magic Decalogue to you because it seemed to care for you?

Far too young and English and full of piss and vinegar to be a Quixote, our Don;
Did all of your intentions make pure your mentions now that they are all gone?

Only one net for the fish which scorned your bait, in the end satiate;
Is this Gospel of Peter abandoned without completion, or finished, or a deletion?

Because Peter is the name of the dead boy I am writing about here;
Vacation contemplation, summer, ardent lover, simple man, yet complex now dead?

Kindness, queer determination, near condemnation, more football player than saint;
What worlds did you touch, how much to deserve, as such what desserts?

The lobster, the beefsteak, for Lord's sake the corn crake breeds far from home.
Why is your laughter fleeting yet stone inscriptions are lasting in the vast fasting?

Crex crex, rex of your forefathers' fields, a brekekekex you heard, here now again though gone;
If that which is null is not zero, where is our grease-smelling hero?

Memory will aid though memory will fade, a lifetime's a unit of measurement;
What pleasure meant, when the day was through, what time is it, and where are you?

—Janet Daily, Point House, August 3, 1980

Six Punctuals

Punctual #499

Norwegian police recovered Munch's The Scream, stolen during 1994 Winter Olympics. Oslo's National Gallery auctioned off the ladder and screwdriver used for the crime. Buyer signed simply "Love, Ed". Do you recognize what this means? Failing to steal his own painting, Munch returned back to hell on earth to collect his tools.

Punctual #490

Budimir Sobat voluntarily held breath underwater just shy of 25 minutes. Controlled environment, Budimir thought. Broken records never occur at useful times, Budimir thought, what if I witnessed beneath ocean waves the entire sinking of the Lusitania, then stayed an extra 5 minutes to rescue passengers? Budimir also held record for Humblest Croatian.

Punctual #314

Natasha Zvereva lost 1988 French Open final in 34 minutes, with rain delay. Uncovered cheesy broccoli pesto pasta paired with lemon pepper chicken cannot cook that quick. Her opponent's service box clay smooth as Nefertiti Bust's crown band. Natasha either slipped or somersaulted into the grain entrapment that day. Hair down danced round the silo Steffi Graf.

Punctual #269

Insane asylum reformer Dorothea Dix's habit of firing nurses she did not personally hire was a hope masterclass. The Cranston, Rhode Island minimum security prison named after her closed. They ran full-time Sabbath and other activities. Swedish Goggles Day comes to mind. Inmates pretended to fill cells with chlorinated water. Guard whistle, lifeguard whistle.

Punctual #412

Chilean Surrealist Gomez Correa spent final 48 seasons in bed paralyzed. Through casement window a Boldo tree grew almost into Gomez's bedroom. Cousins replanted so Gomez could see from a better proximity. The visual shift between Gomez and the Boldo tree became a sunrise rendezvous venue between a tule elk and a silky terrier.

Punctual #68

Tsutomu Yamaguchi designed oil tankers and survived both Hiroshima and Nagasaki bombings. Property owners who thought they made decisions made him laugh. He walked at 93 around unlit gambling dens. When he arrived home, a blind copper pheasant sometimes bumped into a short staff affixed to fifteen bells. Usually that did not happen.

Lucian Staiano-Daniels

Five Tanka

sidewalk
for a long time
after the bleached slats
the desert
which is tameless

kodachrome
red
so vast
i'll squeeze it between my hands
and devour it

upward by upward
black mold along the bottom wall
wicking
fore running
the yama kings that slither beneath the earth

sunrise
early spring
like the first
appearance of mint
on the planet

old woman's cyst
over the lump
moist unwrinkled skin
how powerfully, without a goal
life renews itself

Nineteen Locks

The first came loose with just a touch, and then
The next was just a breath of pollen.
The third took longer, made of sunsets spread
Along a rocky coast. The fourth was open
When you arrived. The fifth lay down a den
Of mulch and mushroom, a tangled maze of dead
Roots, blackened beds, broken desks, cables cut
In ages past. The sixth: an altar, where prayers

Unmade still smoked like candles snuffed. The air
Grew thinner then. The doors behind you shut.
The way ahead was all there was. Rough squares
Were smoothed to spheres for centuries, and there,
The sixth undone, the daunting seventh stood:
A game of chess assembled in the dark.
The eighth through tenth were windings in a wood,
At first all pine, then oak, then birch. A spark

You struck to see ignited leaves. They burned
For days, until horizons showed themselves.
You found unlikely treasures might be earned
In heaps of ash. The next to come: Long shelves
Of books, though they contain a single word.
You had to read them all. It made no sense
Because the letters, strange, remained unheard,
Unpronounceable and thus immense.

Then lifetimes went to clear the rest, the glade,
The plaster masks, a tide of stars, a floor
Of clouds in storm, the bad-dream parts that made
Up spindle, spring, keyway, bolt, and door.
At last, the long, astonishing shadow
You cast across the fields in the first light,
Your shapes and lines, the signs that greet your sight,
Because you're free, with nowhere left to go.

Stefano De Vecchi

Love Poem

translated by Rose Facchini

We are part
of the same desert
and you are my
favorite
grain of sand
it doesn't need to be said
but I think it's clear
When there's a storm
I never lose sight of you

Irene Moccia

Contact Lenses

translated by Rose Facchini

It makes my heart
seethe, your distinct
silence. Your hours are
black with embers: loving
is a waste of time
finally gained.

Fate: a touch. Your palms.
Morning breaks over me.
You opened me, now,
with just the touch of your fingers.

How fragile, gazing at each other
tonight.

ALBAN FISCHER

FROM "HUMAN ARSENAL"

Falling down a well is prohibited.
Those who do fall for hours, for days,
fall out the bottom of the world.
Then the drifting. Eventually, one
gets sucked into the earth's
gravitational pull, back into the
atmosphere, ignites upon reentry.
Barrels ineluctably towards loved ones.
Every day, people scattering the earth over
in an attempt to evade their children,
siblings, dearest compatriots.
Many spend their entire lives
scrambling for shelter—so absurd:
Inevitably, the loved ones make impact.
One bright day when we least expect it.
The force of the hit cratering reality
around us. Reality is pockmarked
from innumerable strikes. One can tread
scarcely a few feet without all life
blinking in and out of view. Some fashion
canes to feel about for the craters.
The incapacitated are the most nimble among us.
Their sign for *well* is made with two hands
embracing a void.

Early AM half-light. A car door is abruptly flung open in our path. A figure leans out, bellows crud onto the sidewalk, closes the door. We catch our reflection in the viscid splotch before hurrying on.

We'd needed to talk, reveal all we'd been holding back for so long. We'd begin, convulse, start over. Finally, we acquiesced to patting each other's backs, croaking, "It's ok, let it out . . . let it out . . ."

A woman had fallen, was struggling to get up, endlessly thrashing in her own guck. We attempted help and too were embroiled. A man appeared, went gif. Soon all simply passed, inculcated, heaving.

You might take this down:
That we have been blown to smithereens.
That we have been complicit in our being blown to smithereens.
That these smithereens create a new kind of comedy,
a comedy in which laughter is not permitted, a comedy that to recognize
     as comedy is deemed inappropriate.
You might take this down.

You might take this down:
That the day is a synecdoche for the nothing that dwarfs it, that the day
is a synecdoche for our rise and fall,
and, further, that it takes the moon a full nanosecond to circle the planet,
     and
that the earth is a synecdoche for all quarriable daylight.
You might take this down.

You might take this down behind the museum and commit wickedness
     upon it,
you might take it down to the water, overburden its extremities, thrust it
     into the deep.
You might stand there on the Paywall, smoking a restorative Camel in the
     cool of dusk,
watching, as it cruelly sinks.

*They'd come to proselytize, clammy-faced, lips crusted, speech
acrid. Could we not see? It is all around us, they say from the stoop.
But the spiel grows unctuous, its thrust diffuse, their footing ungainly.*

*In the park, we witness the children making a game of it: A victim is
chosen, spun to the brink of bursting, while the others dart and shriek,
playing at fear of being made kettle, besmircher, ditto.*

*The crowd. Cries loosened among what is loosed. The dignitary,
beset. The swell become wave, monologue a spume. We glimpse the
news footage through the bodega's filmy splashguard, and shudder.*

You can't break off in the middle of the dream. It's illegal.

After all, one doesn't run down dozens of flights of stairs to arrive nowhere.

Nor does one draft page after page of interoffice memoranda to illustrate the
heuristics of the shovel, the bulldozer.

And one does not suffer such parataxis merely to suffer parataxis. One suffers it
to be crippled by it, to be crippled by it ostentatiously, extravagantly.

It is as though the words burst forth of their own accord, and only come to lie in
their particular sense by chance.

It's all chance—

That one can even dream at all, that the dream can mean or be bent into
meaning,

that the dream can end or be ended.

Not the kind of chance that is blasted at you from the sky with utmost force,

but the kind that flutters around you as fragments in the viscous haze of the
dream.

*We enter the parlor: the chiromancer's rheumy eyes, our heinous
borborygmi. It was foolish to have come: Hands clasped over
mouths, we attempt to stanch the question we can't help but answer.*

*We beware the upper window. Beware the escalator. Beware the
festival, the fair. The theatre, the nightclub. Beware the orator. Beware
the traffic stop, the officer canting ecliptic into the cabin . . .*

*The docent is a happy man. We ogle the vessels cradling mere air,
canvases nuzzling mere gouache, and are happy too, our coveralls
crinkling and squishing, docent intoning dreamily above the din.*

Mike Silverton

Wunderhorn Honks

Cat & Mouse

The cat's impartial,
it vomits on everything.
The mouse offering to help with the dishes,
is it really fair to call it vermin?

Quite

"I've always wanted to be a bird."
"Ah yes."
"They fly, you know."
"Quite."
The men are standing on one foot each.
A third party punctures the bulge on which the pair converse.
I cannot explain why the two men are standing
on one foot each. To know what it feels like to be a flamingo?
The men are in business attire, which is odd.
Their shoes are already under water. From one perspective
the punctured bulge looks like an inverted ladle;
from another, a potted geranium. Spontaneity
becomes difficult.

Mildred

What is this place where
everybody calls each other Mildred
and wears snoods?
One also hears the sputter of guttering candles.
Time is running out.
Pity especially an urchin under an awning
whose grandmother rails, "You goddamn midget!"
Yet the urchin is six-foot eight.
Above the clink of costly stemware
One hears, again, the sputter of guttering candles.
Time is running further out!

The People of Peru

The people of Peru have engaged
in a fabulous human chain from their
loftiest mountaintop to me,
an undeserving honoree
whose tongue, when challenged,
dribbles down his chin

(of course I mean my chin)
like a mouthful of home fries
I chew with my favorite molars,
Alphonse and Gaston.

THREE MEN IN OLD AGE

I shall come to rest as a statue.
Vandals will snap off bits
and I will dwindle.
The proprietor of a cruise ship line
slides about on petroleum jelly.
He seems not to understand.
A pilot flies in so leisurely a fashion
birds alight and peck at his lunch.

MOONLIGHT

Children are threatened by unhappy fathers looking
at their paunches in full-length mirrors. Children
are threatened by patches of moonlight
dotting their bedding.

SOME OF IT WAS LIES

I lured you, smiling, my fingers at your earlobes, flicking.
Pricks fuel up on hills of dreams, pissing
on my half-assed schemes.

Seriously,
can a line exist before it seeks ink, or a pencil, or a chisel?
Should we revert to glyphs? Draw me a picture.
Astonish me.

THE GRIFFON

The griffon with digestive issues, its memory lingers.
As scat on the tablecloth? Likely not.
(So many walls, so few murals.)
Less likely yet, a homing pigeon to which clings
a postage stamp. Even less likely,
a landslide comprised of ground lamb.
From ubiquitous suction, the extraction of Hope,
or possibly the tongue, had the gag
been cosmic. Or a dining-room ceiling
collapsing on one's birthday cake.

Stanley's Questionnaire

What's a ming bean, Stanley?
(Never mind, that's a trick question.)
Who first described crêpes suzette as anguish in drag?
(Shackleton? Wrong.)
Would it help to read a phone book cover to cover?
(It depends? Be specific.)
Should Jesus be blamed for the fabled camel's broken back?
(Yes. But locating the last straw's like looking
for a needle in a haystack.)
Who shot at zeppelins with gobs of narwhal snot?
(Shackleton! Correct!)

My Magic Beans

Was I ever a farmer in blue velvet coveralls?
I don't think so. I really can't remember. So why
do I long for meadows of clover? So why
do I long for a lady called Prunella even on mornings
when redskins wander off with
my magic beans?

What Lunatics!

What lunatics! One picked up another,
over and over, as the Great Grease ever oozed,
which then seemed a low point, but no!
The incoming tide was an Even Greater Grease!

Dearest Caryatid

Dearest Caryatid, I deplore your absence from
my eager arms, especially when you comprise an aspect
of a wall from which you somewhat project.

Mr. X

How luxurious it is to sprawl in the subtropics!
As you'd see were this a picture, I assume
a decubitus posture, albeit half-heartedly, for
I am tempted to arise and punch Mr. X in the head,
that nursery of puerile thought. For example,
the shape in the dark from which Mr. X shrinks is
nothing more ominous than a subtropical lump.
Why don't I tell it to go away?
Because I am otherwise engaged
by the pattern of Mr. X's stagger under
the banana harvester I exchanged
for his hat.

Dewdrop

The Poet is building a seaplane.
He is trying to grow the pontoons on his chest.
Alas, his aero-bosom degrades to hundreds of stumps,
many with their own little eyes and remarkably well informed.

The Poet shakes hands with a veal.
"What lovely lilac needles you have, sweet veal!"
Everything that's moist is part of the Poet's study program.
He can evaporate a dewdrop at twenty meters.

The Poet enters with a sop.
The sop gathers its tripe and departs.

Little Park

Little park that I pass through,
I carry off wee bits of you:
I pluck some trees and scoop up bramble,
as I find you in my ramble,
to weave together my own little nation
where the populace dreams of defenestration—
disciples! vocation!

It's at the Launch disruptions occur at
five second intervals.

Also, before my lips could, a competitor's did.
It makes me feel languid.

A Homesick Man

A homesick man smiles at expensive mammals
that remove his hats.
Three times. In circles.
Or better, pools of cool drool
and bloodshot eyes, none of which is available
to modification.
"So, this is what peace is like."

The Hole I Dug

The hole I dug is of little interest,
but I did unearth some old crockery shards.
The skull must belong to the End-Time zealot
given to muttering "Any day now,"
which I find rather amusing,
especially at dusk.

When (in My Dreams)

When I read my poems aloud
(in my dreams)
armpits grow gardenias.

When I read my poems aloud
(in my dreams)
Valkyrie awaken and hone their dentures.

When I read my poems aloud
(in my dreams)
Jesus cancels the Second Coming.

When I read my poems aloud
(in my dreams)
Orpheus pawns his lyre.

When I read my poems aloud
(in my dreams)
The Urals shout "Tovarisch!"

When I read my poems aloud
(in my dreams)
nails canoodle with four-by-fours.

When I read my poems aloud
(in my dreams)
hairlines recede and flagpoles retract.

When I read my poems aloud
(in my dreams)
objections vanish into cracks.

also

also inaudible poetry during riots, shivarees, earthquakes and air raids.
also Great Moments swanning about the premises.
also nibbled perimeters.
also dragons whose flames no one likes.
also dragoons who show up too late.
also to one's threshold returning as freight.

I Have Dreams

I review my squirrels with excelsior stuffed
even as I hum along to Lauritz Melchior singing
Some Enchanted Evening. I have also gagged on mulch.

Sugar-Free Gesundheit

Someone I know said that poetry is like a pump
for a yet to be invented bicycle.
He also said that poetry is like a bicycle
for a yet to be invented pump.
On another occasion he said that poetry
is like a hole in a basement.
I've given this some thought and have decided—
these are just opinions.

Like an Elf off a Shelf

I fly like an elf off a shelf, like a tooth in a gale,
like Mother Goose, like a petard hoist. So
much to see! So much to touch! Pro
sciutto on focaccia!

Bluemud

Bluemud refers to a style of jazz
for male vocalist, piccolo and cimbalom
(also known as Low-Rent Fru-Fru),
popular in the Chicago area in
the mid-to-late 1930's.
Bluemud is said to be the creation of
Petty-officer first-class Wayning Omen,
who perished at Pearl Harbor aboard the naval tug Chester
A. Arthur, at the time of the Japanese attack.
Recordings of bluemuds are said to have been made in 1938
on the Snappy Happy label, but there seem to be
no copies extant.
Two rather dubious examples
of bluemud lyrics appear in Ray Roussel's
Jazz Aberrations (Philosophical Library, 1948).

On Turning Ninety

A moment to celebrate barrel-aged whiskey,
first aid for a rear-view sensibility.
We poets, we have the chutzpah, and springtime,
it has the birds and the bees. And here am I
who today cries *slainte*!

My Liquid

Who salted my Way to Immortality?
Better than salt,
gold dust.
Better than gold dust,
crocodile tears—
the mention of which makes me wonder,
afresh, about the bite marks
in my liquid.

O Men of America

As I shelter in the shade of a Doctor Pepper billboard,
I observe my fellow Americans fondling bottle stoppers, and
say to myself, Silverton, if you separate a bottle from its stopper
what have you got? Fled effervescence.

As I pause among the season's first asparagus,
I observe my fellow Americans
sniffing and licking their bottle stoppers.
I have nothing to say to myself.

I study the moon.
It looks like a cork. I think for a moment
and say to myself, Silverton, you're no selenologist
and you're no bargain either.

Summertime blows her flugelhorn (mimic, now, a flugelhorn).
Build me, O men of America, a wall so enduring
as to stop the irksome traveler who asks,
"How then is one to inhale your homeland's fragrant zephyrs
or even to proceed with one's nose pressed thus
to an enduring wall?"

Flagpole

I'm pretty sure that's someone else
wondering about those other problems,
looking for handles, looking at the clouds,
remembering to change his socks,
remembering to thank me for
 conducting the octet
with an axle.

Ahoy!

Yes, well,
certainly, but what about
old enemies honing their dentures?

A Successful Poem

Little dale that I pass through
I carry off some bits of you.
I take some trees and patch of sky
to make a homeland by and by.

Yet before I could a stranger said,
"You find me in something edible steeped,
perhaps oyster stuffing. Is this Thanksgiving?"

A successful poem
is like moonbeams on a bowl of soup.
A successful poem
makes amethysts of zits.
A successful poem
is like a hummingbird examining a teaspoon.
A successful poem
never runs out of words.

Effective Curses

Effective curses leave no trace.
Goldsmiths working filigree do more
discernible damage. One says this to oneself
on undermined pavement and drops into a pit filled
with ocarinas (or misshapen yams).

Grit Is an Expression of Abundance

And if his mantle should shelter in a tree
and snarl at the poet attempting to retrieve it?
Would he be discouraged or richer for the experience?
Is a ladder involved? Silken perhaps?
Do I ask too many questions?

Like Mayonnaise

And his acolytes, O how they wept!
Through their tears they admitted, well yes,
he burned with hate as a permanent state.
They admitted, well yes, he never walked but strode,
yammering on about provisions.
"I guess I'll be a cold cut soon, exiled as I am
on this baguette-shaped promontory."
And his acolytes, the tears they shed tasted
like mayonnaise.

Flotsam Poem

Is it inappropriate, returning to one's
birthplace hammering on
a brake drum?

Fond Thoughts

My feet are not good looking.
I celebrate them, rather,
as transportation to love. I loft,
too often enraptured,
and fall too soon to earth,
fond hopes scattered like shattered
flamingos. Several appear at the kitchen door.
My mother mistakes them for
a dog she loathes.

Walnuts

The causeway lay uneasy
with its sinister moods and tantrums.
Walnuts might have played a part.

One turns off the light.
One feels about the darkened room
for walnuts. One encounters sticky wads
where none had ever been.

The poet puts down an empty stein.
He sighs. He presses his fists to
his rheumy eyes. Outside,
the clopity-clop of a horse's hooves.
A bone-weary overseer is returning from
a walnut expanse. And out the door the poet flies,
with walnuts. From the darkened room,
a booming voice. "Stop! Freeze!
Install a period!
Like so: (.)"

Perhaps upon Perhaps

Never so grand as a thunder clap, but
a thought even so, perhaps about impermanence,
perhaps about a ghost you saw. Perhaps it's someone
else's thought sticking a finger in your ear. Perhaps upon perhaps,
let's also be concerned by what we suspect is clandestine
mirth. Rudy, get your ass off that mountain!

A Poet's Melancholy

A poet's melancholy reads like a sandwich board,
"I'm Distraught Avoid Contact
But Contributions Always Welcome."
In anticipation of your question, yes, a brassiere,
also arithmetic, as I am growing an all-terrain vehicle.
And really, how fine a thing it is for a fellow
to have gone through his repertory of lengthy echoes.
(Rudy, get your ass of that mountain!)

Concubines Depart

Maman so enjoyed random gestures!
Allow me to explain. I had a pangolin that produced a lump
I named Mystery (the lump, not the pangolin). Laughter
quickly turned to respect. Prosperity soon followed.
Yet mon père was too quick to cry Oncle!
to any crevasse from which a threat
might some day emerge.

Indoors, worse, afflictions everywhere—
perils smirking, evening descending with its onesies on.
Some unnamed stupidity blows in from
a window. Concubines depart,
as do goods and
services.

Significance

What is significant? What is its measure?
A passerby in sweat socks to which cling burdock seeds
provides no occasion for interest. He succumbs
moments later to milkweed pollen. We need to acquire
black armbands. We need to brush our teeth.
The sky above sees nothing. Dunkel ist das Leben,
ist der Tod.

One Loose Feather

Too much debris, too many wild geese,
too many unreliable edges, and who asked for these
phosphorescent ashes, quite by definition
dangerous, regrettably unremarkable friends,
one loose feather, probably mislaid,
a third person crouching behind a sofa,
quite by definition sinister, and who in the world
could possibly enjoy these January windows?

Or a Fish

On a shelf, dimly lit, my tongue, Auteur. Warm
and wet, it glistens like a bayonet.
Or a fish.

I am pale. In fact I am ill. My tongue lies
on a plate like a length of
flank steak.

My tongue has a mind of its own. It enjoys licking
monuments. It prefers the taste of
verdigris.

Twelve Lines, Halved

The trees sway beguilingly though
not necessarily poetically. From a distance
they seem benevolent. From a greater distance
they look like broccoli. One needs to be close to hear
the trees whispering, Go home. Summer's upon us
and you're in the way.

It isn't enough to fill the reader's heart with a love
of mystery: Pineapples! Each morning
another slashed cousin! The poet must cajole.
The poet must reveal available alternatives.
The poet must write, poetically of course,
about forestry's prospects.

But Only in This Poem

Soggy sandals and smashed potatoes,
is that any way to begin a poem?
Well yes, like now.
I could have begun with Greetings all!
to everything I see, including the odd mirage.
A levitating man (but only in this poem),
is possibly dangerous. Now he is hovering at
some dimly lit distance. I become apprehensive
(but only in this poem). Elsewhere I remove doorknobs
from under readers' noses for no better reason than
a few extra lines (but only in this poem).

My Sweet Muse

she sings in the conditional.
My sweet muse,
she takes me everywhere.
To honor her endeavors, some
trav'ling music, my
strophe.

Another Flotsam Poem

Have you noticed the figs? I like to think they make
me look good. How about the waterfall
I never hide behind?

Quintain

How to be odder in an age of odd façades:
Tree-ring cellulite, legs that vanish
and return without notice,
women's behinds on one's mind
as an excuse for fleeing on ice skates.

Helpful, Useful and Informative Couplets

I ask you, is stuffing a deceased taxidermist fitting?
How and where should he be mounted?

I am the spawn of a cumulus cloud!
I humidify arrivistes!

You come to me with eruptions. I repair you. Neither
swiftly not slowly does it snow in Gabon.

As a break from spreading rumors,
I enter summer rentals and leave teapots.

It is strange, seeing nothing everywhere
nor caring that certain beverages taste like masonry.

"You have a look I once found alarming."
Nature abhors cosmetic enigmas.

My disapproval of the Treaty of Ghent raises questions.
I see you but don't see you, if you take my meaning.

I just met the other loneliest man in the world
but he is crazy and doesn't count.

Intent on diction I fail to note how mere steps away
Behemoth practices somersaults.

Are we merely perishables asking to be disposed of
thoughtfully? I'm told the psyche smells.

I'm content enough here in bed
yet long to know what kites are thinking.

Empty a down-filled pillow over a pond.
Confuse the fish.

Choose one: lilies wilting in a crypt, a wife in a bathroom
singing loudly, an octopus with a knife.

I rearrange traffic from my office in the bank, with a paddle.
They're always there, these vehicles.

Summer ends. I return to the house. Apples
remain, devoted to their trees.

One day long ago I preened and pouted
and sat in a bucket. One day later I wondered why.

"Keep me supplied!" I shout from the keyboard.
"Inaccuracies are welcome."

The no-accident bonus clause makes for tepid adventurers.
Thus one avoids dark rooms and crevasses.

In 1714 Daniel Fahrenheit invented a thermometer
you could spit out in the doctor's office.

A man plants a crown of thorns on his glans
and says, mostly to himself, "Jesus! That hurts!"

Buried in delta sludge, J. Edgar Hoover's avatar
tries to think of something amusing.

Remind yourself during the pageant that these
these are mere bullets and that you're a Rosicrucian.

States of grace etch goose eggs against a sky-blue sky.
A visiting committee opts for dignity.

Finally, there is the abduction scene.
Today the sky is cloudy gray.

The Litania /Litany by Giorgio Caproni. Untranslatable?

The poet, critic and translator Giorgio Caproni (1912–1990) was born in Livorno, Tuscany—once known by the English as Leghorn—and he lived most of his adult life in Rome. Yet he moved with his family to Genoa in 1922 and spent the rest of his childhood and early adulthood in that city. Although he did write about Livorno, his place of birth, his name is associated with the city of Genoa.

As a young English poet teaching at the University of Genoa in the 1980s I was keen to find a way into Italian poetry. It wasn't easy. The kind of poetry I had known as a student in England—Philip Larkin, the Liverpool Poets, the Beat Poets, American confessional poets such as Lowell and Plath as well as Frank O'Hara from the New York School for example—didn't have any equivalence in Italian.

To worship at the altar of Italian poetry seemed rather like attending high mass on a holy day with all the trimmings—incense, Latin supplications, priestly garments, knee bending. The first literary event I attended in Italy was a reception for the Florentine poet Mario Luzi (1914–2005). In that hushed and reverential room it felt as if a literary god had dropped by to rest his wings and take a little nourishment from his adoring acolytes. Any discussion of poetry at the university threw up the word *ermetico* or hermetic in a flash. I knew post-war neorealism had pushed back against the 'impenetrability' of the hermetic style both on the screen and on the page yet in the classrooms the old brigade still ruled the roost: Giuseppe Ungaretti (1888–1970), Salvatore Quasimodo (1901–1968), Eugenio Montale (1896–1981).

Montale, after all, was a Ligurian poet and furthermore he had received the Nobel Prize. No doubt seized by a visceral clutch I sometimes passed the house in which he was born: 'Il Poeta Eugenio Montale Nacque in Questa Casa, Il 12 Ottobre, 1896.' The house is in Corso Dogali.

Not long after the beginning of my lengthy sojourn in Genoa (or Zena in the local dialect) a mature student of mine invited me for dinner. No doubt we ate trofie with pesto, followed by fish. During dinner she presented me—rather ceremoniously—with an annotated copy of Montale's *Ossi de Seppia* (*Cuttlefish Bones*)—published in 1925. No easy read! I felt as if I'd been inducted into the Knights Templar. I was both honoured and touched but I didn't feel I was really cut out for the role.

During the fascist years (1922–1945), in order to throw the authorities off their scent, it was easy to see why poets might cloak their work in opaque manoeuvres and linguistic complexity. Yet as a young Englishman now based in Genoa I wanted to find an Italian poet whose writing resonated with my own experience of living in that remarkable, dilapidated city.

Caproni came to the rescue. My Italian was improving and Caproni's poetry was approachable. There's the risk, of course, that in celebrating his engagement with named streets and named piazzas that one fails to recognise the metaphysical fiat which quickens much of his writing. Simplicity, so-called, can be beguilingly misleading. Important to remember too that Caproni was a partisan during the Second World War (in Val Trebbia/Liguria) and much of his earlier poetry is mindful of Italy's tortured history. Nevertheless I was delighted to read about places I might pass on my way to work or piazzas where I might drink coffee with friends and colleagues.

I need to say something about the morphology and/or lay-out of Genoa because Caproni is a poet who is alive to the particular atmosphere of Liguria's capital city. Historically it's always been wrapped around the port. Genoa was a leading sea power in the medieval period, rivalling and sometimes getting one over Venice. The old city or *centro storico*—dripping with exhausted grandeur—is the biggest extant medieval centre in Europe, a veritable labyrinth, whose *vicoli* (the narrowest of streets) might themselves be viewed as the lines of a poem forever seeking appropriate form. After which the hills which take you up to elegant Castelletto and far beyond with its ancient forts. Genoa is not a bicycle city. Making one's way around the place inevitably involves lifts and funiculars and steep climbs up and down the *carrugi* and *creuze*. The Genoese have strong calf muscles and doughty legs. The physical act of ascending and descending as you criss-cross the city, dipping in and out of sunlight, creates a quasi-Dantean metaphysic. I always felt Genoa—the city against the sea or, more magnificently, La Superba—was a world unto itself. It was unique yet it was not without a wider symbolic valency.

Before turning to Caproni's *Litania* I would like to refer quickly to his poem 'L'Ascensore' ('The Lift /Elevator'). In Piazza Portello, just off Via Garibaldi, which Thomas Hardy described as the most beautiful street in Europe, you can catch the lift to Castelletto. Soon enough you step onto the *Spianata* to be greeted with a panoramic view of the sea and the city spread out along the coast. Poet and poem are immortalised in lapidary manner on the wall near the lift itself. These are the opening lines:

Quando andrò in paradiso
non voglio che una campana
lunga sappia di tegola
all'alba—d'acqua piovana.

Quando mi sarò deciso
d'andarci, in paradiso
ci andrò con l'ascensore
di Castelletto, nelle ore
notturne, rubando un poco
di tempo al mio riposo.

Caproni's work, in general, has not been widely translated into English. In Jamie McKendrick's *The Faber Book of 20th Century Italian Poems* (2004), for example, Caproni is represented by three short poems. I have located a translation of 'L'Ascensore' on the Poetry Foundation site. This is how Michael Palma deals with the opening stanzas:

When I go to paradise
let there be only one
bell, scented with rainwater
and with tiled roofs at dawn.

When I decide to go
to paradise, I will go

there in the elevator,
at night, of Castelletto,
stealing a little piece
of my eternal peace.

All Genoese know how to find the lift to Castelletto; most Genoese will know about the poem, or at least the poem's opening. When the moment comes to pack your bags you might attach your celestial wings and take the lift—or in effect be lifted up– to that paradisal place on the hill. It's a brilliant conceit. It's as if the poem has been bolted onto the city itself. Yet in actual fact the piece is a rather creative obituary for the poet's beloved mother Anna Picchi. Now a schoolteacher in Rome, Caproni came back to Genoa in 1948 to visit his mother only to discover she was nearing the end of her life. Later in the poem, having reached Castelletto in the dark, the poet wonders if he'll recognise his mother in the lamplight. If he does, he says, they'll stand together at the iron railing

alone and hand in hand,
betrothed as we had never
been in all those years.
In the shudder of the railing.

Dreamlike, ghostly, heartrending, the poem is almost unbearably sentimental in a very Italian way. Years later when I was living in Castelletto myself—a kind of geographical promotion if you like—I had to take St Anna's Funicular, rather than the lift, to get to and back from work. At some point I wrote 'St Anna's Funicular'. On my part an early nod to the great Caproni:

When I go down to hell
I will take St Anna's Funicular.
It will be waiting for me
in the nearly dark of a
velvet-skied Genoese evening.

I will be the only passenger
and the doors will slide shut
with a sublime finality.
It will be quite an occasion,
this journey into eternity.

And in that narrow steep descent
I will be given my last vision
of the city against the sea
and I will pass lighted windows
full of comfort and chandeliers.

Of all his Genoese poems *Litania/Litany* most perfectly *writes* the city. Probably written in 1952 it's an ambitious poem not least because of its length (45 stanzas, mostly quatrains, some 180 lines in all) and its virtuoso use of an AABB rhyme scheme, with an anaphoric drum beat. If I were to attempt a translation the rhyme scheme would have to be reconsidered or abandoned. To non-speakers of Italian the poem is not completely inaccessible. Italian is a phonetic language so one can speak it as it is written (unlike English) and thus it is possible hear the sharp rhyme again and again. The English poet Charles Tomlinson, who lived in Liguria, was well versed in Italian poetry including that of Caproni. Tomlinson argues: 'The chances of rhyme are like the chances of meeting—/In the finding fortuitous, but once found, binding.' Those who are interested in Caproni's poem might listen to various readings/recordings on the internet/YouTube. The title of the Caproni's piece is instructive. The structure is constant; kinetically repetitive. And in each stanza Genoa—or *Genova*—is called upon twice. Ninety times in the poem as a whole. The city is variously apostrophised, celebrated, fetishised, sometimes cursed. From the beginning:

> Genova mia città intera.
> Geranio. Polveriera.
> Genova di ferro e aria,
> mia lavagna, arenaria.
>
> Genova città pulita.
> Brezza e luce in salita.
> Genova verticale,
> vertigine, aria scale.

The panoramic, encyclopaedic intentions of the poem are revealed in that first line: 'Genoa my entire city'. The reader is taken on a tour through the city and beyond. Naturally a Ligurian reader will be familiar with the landscape of the poem notwithstanding the fact Caproni's poem was written in the 1950s. Place names, a Capronian speciality, include Castelletto, Caricamento, Albaro, Borgoratti, Sestri, Fontane Marose, Voltri, Sturla, Marassi, Sottoripa, Stalgieno, the famous cemetery and/or necropolis, Genoa's iconic city of the dead.

In the second stanza we find 'Genova verticale,/vertigine, aria scale', namely a laconic description of that very dynamic I spoke of in my introduction to 'The Lift/Elevator'. Vertical

Genoa, giddying Genoa, a city whose steep walkways haul you up into the very air itself.

Caproni's *Litania* employs concrete nouns and proper nouns generously. Reading the poem becomes a physical /somatic experience. At a psychological level it is also a poem of reconstruction. Genoa was heavily bombed in the war. It is said of Philip Larkin and his fellow travellers in the Movement that their celebration of premodernist traditional forms in their quest to restore the English line was analogous with the rebuilding of British cities after the destruction of the Luftwaffe. Caproni, too, remembers in stanza 43 the Genoa of '*Bombardamenti*'.

> Genova di lamenti.
> Enea. Bombardamenti.
> Genova disperata,
> invano da me implorata.

It's easy here to see here how '*Bombardmenti*' is followed by '*Genova disperata*' (city of desperation) and '*implorata*' (imploration, in vain, *invano*.) What is really fascinating is the reference to *Enea*/ Aeneas of Virgilian fame. The statue is still found in Piazza Bandiera which was bombed during the war. The statue survived and becomes for Caproni a poetic talisman. The poems discussed in this article are both found in his collection *Il Passaggio d'Enea* (1956). Aeneas survived the fall of Troy and made his way to Italy becoming an important ancestor of Romulus and Remus, mythical creators of Rome. Aeneas might be said to represent defiance and, ultimately, hope.

In fact Caproni's *Litany* enjoys a post-fascist 'democratic' spirit as it celebrates the observable and pragmatic not to mention the growing power of the Italian left. This is of particular relevance to Genoa. It celebrates, in great part, ordinariness, the quotidian, and craftsmanship, working class labour and artistic prowess. There are references to slate, to building sites, ship building, to the port, dockers, ships, fishing, sex workers, conscripted soldiers, the hinterland with its partisan traditions and the '*Genova di violino*', a reference to Paganini and Caproni's own love of music. Noteworthy that '*Genova di violino*' rhymes, ironically, with '*topo*' (rats) and '*casino*' (mess/chaos). All of this creates a tangibility that sets Caproni's poetic against the abstractions of his predecessors who were of a hermetic persuasion. Caproni is conscious of what might be called a Ligurian line—he refers to the Genoa of 'Campana. Montale. Sbarbaro' (stanza 15), yet he is qualifying it here. Craft and clarity rather than modernist experimentation are foregrounded.

For all its locked in, quasi-gnomic economy, the poem is fraught with emotion. Consider stanzas 3 and 4:

Genova nera e bianca.
Cacumine. Distanza.
Genova dove non vivo,
mio nome, sostantivo.

Genova mio rimario.
Puerizia. Sillabario.
Genova mia tradita,
rimorso di tutta la vita.

The third stanza refers to the 'black and white' colour of the city thanks to the historical use of marble and slate. Yet 'black and white' might also suggest in a city whose buildings reach skywards, unlike Venice say, how sunlight can suddenly open up a dark piazza, as if there were some kind of binary opposition between the forces of good and something more sinister. Genoa is, by nature, a melancholic city and in 1857 Herman Melville noted in his diary that from above, with its forts and wild hinterland, Genoa seemed like the fortified camp of Satan ready to do battle with the archangels. In the medieval period, incidentally, Genoa had the largest slave markets in Europe.

In the third stanza Caproni uses the Latin word 'Cacumine' which might be described as a peak or summit, something *in extremis*, which again not only inscribes Genoa's mountainous geography but also suggests perhaps some kind of overwhelming agony: the city on the hill now becoming a type of calvary. The third line of the third stanza reminds us that this evocation of Genoa is being written by a poet who no longer lives there—*Genova dove non vivo*—a poet in exile. And whereas the fourth stanza (anticipating the end of the poem) refers to the city as his rhyming factory it collapses into '*Genova mia tradita,/rimorso di tutta la vita*'—namely a city betrayed by the poet himself, a city, therefore, of lifelong remorse and suffering. The guilt and longing of the poet in exile is speaking here. He is doubtless re-membering the loss of his mother; he is remembering the loss of his childhood and youth; he is remembering the war years which took him away from the city.

Caproni's *Litany* is an emotional lever for Ligurians. Giorgio Caproni 'is one of theirs' which is not dissimilar to their adoration of Fabrizio De André (1940–1999). Notwithstanding his wealthy upbringing, De André became '*il cantautore degli emarginati*', the singer-songwriter for the marginalised. His music still haunts the backstreets of the city rather in the way Caproni takes us in stanza 29 to the '*Genova di Sottoripa./Emporio. Sesso. Stipa./Genova di Porta Soprana,/d'angolo e di puttana*':the Genoa of the Sottoripa, and shops and sex and throngs of people and the Genoa of Porta Soprana with its street corners and street walkers. Useful to think of the singer-songwriter and jazz player Paolo Conte too. He's not Genoese but one of his most famous songs is 'Genova Per Noi' ('Genoa for Us'). When he plays in the city the audience demands it and they get to their feet and weep and cheer. Conte says, '*Genova, dicevo, è un'idea come un'altra*', 'Genoa, I was saying, is an idea like any other' but the reason the Genoese love the song is because they know that Conte *knows* that Genoa is not like anything else or anywhere else at all—there's something strange, mysterious and alluringly phantasmagoric about it.

Caproni's *Litany* is about loss of place as well as the recollection of it and the restoration of it. In that sense it works as a form of 'nostos'. It is the poem for Genoese exiles (there are so many nowadays); it might be a poem for sailors and seafarers. My once father-in-law spent much of his life at sea dreaming of his return to Genoa. Caproni's *Litany* is an act of nostalgia, a supplication, a great list, a funeral song, a prayer, joyous, humorous, wry, bitter, unbearably sad, full of lamentation and yearning, or *struggimento*. The Ligurians are known for their *mugungni*. A form of moaning and/or complaining, both existential and banal, and Caproni's *Litany* seems to incorporate something of this too. This is his '*Genova di lamenti*'.

The last stanza, number 45, slips out from under the 4-line carapace to become a little longer; a flourish, of sorts, at the end.

Genova di tutta la vita.
Mia litania infinita.
Genova di stocafisso
e di garofano, fisso
bersaglio dove inclina
la rondine: la rima.

The poem signs off with yearning, with lyrical pulse.

Genoa my entire life.
My infinite litany.
Genoa of stockfish
and carnations,
my target where
the swallow tilts: rhyme.

If the piece begins with 'Genoa my entire city' it concludes with 'Genoa of my entire life/. Infinite litany.' Stepping away from the abstract once again Caproni gives us stockfish and carnations. Stockfish/dried cod is used to make baccalà, rather as you find in Portugal. It is another Genoese dish full of 'emotion' which reminds us of the city's seafaring history. In the Italian '*la rondine*' (swallow) alliterates with' *la rima*' (rhyme). In effect, at the very end of the poem, the switch of the swallow aligns itself with the luminosity of the rhyme.

I was surprised some years ago to find that the Italian scholar Luigi Surdich had cited my poem 'City of Malefic Angels' in *Genova Ch' E Tutto Dire* (2011). His book—a commentary with photographs—is a study of Caproni's *Litany*; the title itself comes from a line in the poem. I was delighted to find that he had described me as a 'capronista'. The poem in question was first published in *The Red Zone* (2007). I was no longer liv-

ing in Genoa yet hardly a day went by without my thinking about the place. Caproni wrote his poem in the 1950s. I was responding to it circa 2005, and thinking of my life in the Ligurian city in the 1980s and 1990s. The Genoese litany therefore unfolds; infinite litany. I share a few lines below:

City of my several corpses
City of light summery Italian waltzes
City of rhyme, city of slime
City of lifts, funiculars and strange
    particulars
City of Caproni and all that baloney
City of my broken knee
City located precariously on the curve of the
    sea

[. . .]

City of the mind gone wrong, De André, city
    of song
City of revisionist historians and,
    increasingly city of Ecuadorians
City of loose ends and long-toothed friends
City of Rina, I wish I'd seen her one more
    time

[. . .]

City of Via Gramsci and my estranged wife
    the banshee
City of the ghetto, Jack, William and
    Castelletto
City of Sampdoria and permanently
    deferred euphoria
City of Valery, Dickens, Montale, Melville
    and Hardy
City of green sauce, city of my not yet
    completed and expensive divorce.

.

REVIEW | David Rose

The Crib and Other Stories
Albertine Sarrazin,
translated by Sonya Moor
Confingo Publishing, 2025

In 1965, an unknown Albertine Sarrazin had two novels published almost simultaneously—*L'Astragale* and *La Cavale*—to wild acclaim. In 1966, *La Cavale* was awarded the prix des Quatre Jurys (Femina, Renaudot, Goncourt, Interallié).

Both novels were translated into English (American), and published by Grove Press in 1967. A penniless Patti Smith bought a copy of *Astragal*, which she declared life-changing, referring to Sarrazin as "her Albertine". Lucia Berlin also became a fan, making a "pilgrimage" in Sarrazin's footsteps. By then, Sarrazin was dead, at twenty nine, from a botched operation on her kidneys; a premature end to a life that itself reads like a synopsis of a novel—a life helpfully laid out in more detail in the Biographical Outline that concludes this book.

Born in 1937 in Algeria, abandoned as a baby; at age 2, adopted by a middle aged military doctor and his wife; at 10, brought by them to France (and raped by an older man); receives a privileged education in a private Catholic girl's school; her rebellious nature results in her adoptive father (who later revoked the adoption) committing her to a reformatory, from which she escaped to pursue a life of petty crime, prison sentences, prostitution, and furious writing.

At age 20, a jailbreak results in a broken astragal bone, which has multiple consequences: she is helped by a lorry driver (and criminal himself) who becomes her accomplice and later her husband; the novel born from that accident is the one Smith reads.

The stories were written mostly in 1962/63—after the novels—and while in prison in Amiens; they are all set in that prison environment, and describe it in detail.

The opening lines of the first story, "The Launderer", preempt an instinctive apprehension at that limited perspective:

"Prison, boring?

"I can assure you, I'm never bored. In general service, you don't get a minute to yourself . . ."

It goes on to to detail a typical day of prison routine, i.e. *every* day's routine. The coping mechanism is to actively seek work, by taking on orderly's tasks, and make them last, hanging it out. Each story is thus a drawn-out account of the minutiae of that routine, and at some length. If that seems offputting, a strong case can be made for persevering.

Consider what miracles Beckett achieved with the mathematics of his sucking stones in mitigation of life's ennui, or of the routines in *Godot,* in which, of course, "nothing happens, *twice."* Sarrazin pulls off the same trick with similar resource: a strongly idiosyncratic voice and sardonic wit.

Her voice is a product of her upbringing: a privileged education, and her rejection of that for a life of petty crime, plus a penchant for crossword puzzles. The result is a mix of upper class French and street- and prison-slang, larded with puns and foreign borrowings; much like Beckett's erudite tramps. It's very witty.

She also makes use of every small deviation in routine, such as the arrival of a new inmate. And

although the setting remains the the same, Sarrazin rings the changes in structure in each story. "Bibiche", for example, is told by three voices, each commenting on the others: a warder, introduced as Madame, later more personally as Matuchette; Bibiche, the stand-in for Sarrazin; and Dufour, an older inmate who becomes friend and "mother" to Bibiche. So we have a narrative triptych, multiple perspectives.

"The Holy Joe Affair" begins with the return to prison of Mary, a prematurely aged recidivist, and revolves around the difficulties of procuring a decent cup of coffee—the Holy Joe of the title, "cup of Joe" being slang I hadn't come across before, "holy" in that it is enjoyed, at its best, as a secular communion between close friends. There is an intricacy to getting that coffee at its best, even at its second or third best. Simplest is to "canteen" (buy with one's personal cash allowance) the approved brand of ground coffee, Legal, and a portable stove, brewing it in one's cell, strained through a handkerchief and generally tepid. Better is to bribe Mary, with a share of one's ground coffee, to make it for you, Mary now ensconced as an orderly in the laundry, with its stove for heating starch and thus access to boiling water. Even then, one has to tactfully supervise Mary's abbreviated percolation method to obtain any strength and taste. The plot, if it can be called that, involves the discovery that Mary has been receiving a superior brand of coffee from the warders and keeping it to herself. The narrator and her friend find the stash, substitute their own Legal, and look forward to brewing a cup that evening, each in her cell but together in that communion, of "an unspeakably good cup, a holy Blessed Joe". It's a long story but fascinating in its intricacies of prison life and politics.

The last—title—story is, for me, the best, because the most structured, and shortest. It's also the most personally revealing, a monologue about the making of a Nativity crib, over a single day. The detailed description of the making, from salvaged scraps, and the ingenuity involved, structures the story satisfyingly tightly while allowing for those personal asides and digressions.

The collection ends with "Journey To Tunis", really an essay rather than story, and directly autobiographical. The journey was made by Sarrazin after being awarded that prize for *La Cavale*—the *prix de Quatre Jurys*, presented in Tunis. Unburdened by the need for storytelling, her prose is on holiday, as she is. It's sharply observant, witty, self-deprecating. She jokes, for example, after the newspapers, having tipped her to win, had changed their minds, that she was resigned to not winning: ". . . Besides, I never could soften up a jury, let alone four! . . ."

So much wit, zest and joy in life makes her death months later unbearably poignant. The zest is there throughout her work; the same impetuosity in life was also how she wrote—headlong, with little or no correction or revision. The novels were only published after extensive editing and cutting (Simone de Beauvoir requested such with a view to recommending the mss. to Gallimard—whether she did so isn't clear, and it was Pauvert that published them). The stories didn't receive the same editorial attention; they were published posthumously by her husband, presumably as the mss. were left.

But despite the impression sometimes of overwriting, with too much detail, it is, as I have said, worth persevering. Prison life drags; no detail of life in an enclosed environment is superfluous (remember Beckett's "closed-space" stories), and the characterization is the stronger for these details; they are fully rounded characters—allowed to *be*.

I was reminded most strongly of the stories of Nelson Algren's in *The Neon Wilderness*—similar environment (the Police lock-up), similar cast; most crucially, a similar "literary lilt and sensuality" (to quote Tom Carson). Algren believed that to strip the writing of those resources in order to achieve a more "authentic", grittier characterization was to condescend, to render his subjects doubly cheated—once by life, again by literature.

Algren, for all his empathetic commitment, was nonetheless writing from the outside, Sarrazin from the inside, literally, and of her peers.

In her world, there was animosity at times, but certainly no condescension. Nor is the reader allowed any.

Inevitably, perhaps, comparisons were made in France at the time with Genet, but there was more than marketing gimmickry in the comparison. There was a (possibly unconscious) Existentialist commitment to freedom in Sarrazin's petty thefts and rebellions; certainly a naive, innate sense of honesty, a furious belief in truth above convention, that could be described as religious. Moor has stated elsewhere that Sarrazin's early writings to her unknown birth mother almost read like prayers. And with as autofictional a writer as Sarrazin, it is not possible to separate life from work—those qualities show through in all she wrote.

There is a very informative Translator's Note as introduction to the collection, worth reading for its insight into the difficulties faced by Moor, especially with the slang—nothing dates faster—but also with precise prison terms. Moor's choices are always assured, fluid, convincing. Sometimes they're inspired. One example will suffice: a description of a used plate left in a cell, containing "congealed beef fat and (Fr.) *autres reliefs*". Moor renders this "congealed beef fat and other bas-reliefs". That "bas-reliefs" is genius.

Such genius won't be surprising if we have read Moor's own work, in her collection *The Comet and Other Stories*—I recommend you do. The title story in particular is miraculously assured in every detail. Comparing the two collections, we see a contrast between Sarrazin's autofictional impetuosity and Moor's cool appraisal coming from artistic maturity. We need both, delight in both.

What we have, then, courtesy of Confingo, is an engaging, stridently witty voice brought back to life, and a major new voice beginning to emerge.

We also have, on the cover of *The Crib*, one of the best designs I have ever come across, courtesy of Zoë McLean.

REVIEW | Mike Silverton

Pink Dust
Ron Padgett
New York Review Books Poets, 2025

The thing about Ron Padgett's poetry I find most engaging is its diction's lucidity—you could as easily call it simplicity—as concoctions of surreal delight, which he crafts with a feather-light touch. An example:

A haiku went up into a tree
and sat there on a limb
it had just made up.

As to the collection's title:

There used to be an eraser
in the shape of a wheel, pink,
attached to a little brush, black,
for erasing pencil words
and then brushing away the residue,
a little pink dust, . . .

I remember these erasers. Do they still exist? (They do. Amazon offers them as collectibles,

$19.50.) Padgett's pink dust calls to mind a monumentally huge eraser with brush by approximate contemporaries, Claes Oldenburg and Coosje van Bruggen, dating from 1999, Typewriter Eraser, Scale X. Padgett's an old guy who, to this older guy's great satisfaction, labels one of the book's three sections Geezer. The other two are Residue and Lockdown. Another pleasure from Geezer:

I put some stamps
on the envelope, maybe enough,
I don't know.
The Post office
should accept it
as is, because
I made an effort.
The post office should look
at the envelope and say
"Well, he made an effort."

Indeed. Padgett's published work goes back to the Sixties. *Pink Dust* is the most recent of an enormous queue, though I doubt it's the last. I wish us both long life and health.

REVIEW | Charles Holdefer

Where I Went Wrong
David Galef
Regal House, 2025

The wisecracking narrator of David Galef's *Where I Went Wrong* has made his share of mistakes in life—probably more than his share, if such things could be quantified. Tony Mazza, the novel's garrulous New Jersey antihero, does not sugarcoat his failures but he often jokes about them. This humorous tale of a man who drifts from job to job and through two marriages is less a journey toward self-knowledge than a catalogue of errors, a sort of blundersroman.

The title of the novel also serves as a catchphrase repeated throughout the story, as Tony muses about his missteps. Chapters are arranged in reverse chronological order, starting in the year 2000 and going back to Tony's birth in 1959, before culminating in a coda returning to the beginning (or end?) of his tale. Causality in Tony's

world is not neat and tidy. "I hate the word *closure*," he ruefully observes. "It's used by people who never get any."

From chapter to chapter, the reader discovers Tony in various guises. He's an aspiring bike racer or real estate broker, a bartender or a hilariously disastrous hospital orderly. He struggles to be a credible parent with his children, endures an abusive father, and most difficult of all, he confronts the tragic disappearance of his younger sister, Angela.

At its core, though, *Where I Went Wrong* is a novel of friendship. Sandy Quade has been Tony's pal since early boyhood, and he pops up at all stages in Tony's life. Sandy refers to Tony as his "little bro." But their friendship is problematic. Sandy is the kind of companion who is always there for Tony in times of trouble, often because he was the reason Tony got into trouble in the first place. Here's how Tony sees Sandy:

"If I were a woman, I'd say [his] chuckle was seductive. That chuckle got us into Checkers Bar in Fulton when we were sixteen. Ha *ha*. Fake ID that Sandy eventually sold to Derek Mahoney, though

Derek got caught. Sandy never does. Ha *ha*. A genius for getting into places he doesn't belong, laughing all the way."

Sandy plays Huckleberry to Tony's Tom. His high spirits offer a solace from the dysfunction of Tony's early home life. In time, though, youthful shenanigans give way to adult fuckups, and instead of Huck and Tom, the stakes shift to something more akin to Harry Lime and Holly Martins in *The Third Man*. Friendships can be dangerous—especially the oldest, seemingly happiest ones.

This aspect of *Where I Went Wrong* stands out, for me, as the novel's most interesting feature.

Tony's descriptions of failed marriages and troubled home life are well-observed and unexceptionable, but they also feel like familiar territory, of a perplexed masculinity trying to cope. Whereas the scenes with Sandy are more vulnerable, and touch a deeper hurt.

The final chapter contains a startling revelation, which will invite the reader to reconsider much of what preceded. Galef is a skilled writer who is highly attuned to the lies we tell each other, and to the lies we tell ourselves.

REVIEW | Jacek Blaszkiewicz

Surface Studies: The Topographical Readings of Mike Corrao
Mike Corrao
Action Books, April 2024

Big books are safe books. No one questions a commuter wielding a thick volume. Big books make good bankers. They nestle bills and conceal the wallet, phone, or whatever else bulges from your pants (David Foster Wallace writes that "dictionaries tend to be hard on the lap," but who commutes with a dictionary). Weaponlike, they are rarely wielded for their inherent blunt mass. Have you ever thrown a big book? It's a chaotic sight. Tap a big book and you will hear the hollow thud of a sourdough loaf. Scrape it against your lips and it will not cut you. Big books are lazy, preferring to press butterfly wings or stop a door or adorn a desk. Sensitive to dust, they wear jackets. Those who carry them have safety in numbers. They go to places where other people carry the same flailing, lazy, sensitive book.

Slim books are the scary ones. They do not frequent book clubs. They have velocity, and velocity is the medium of both poetry and politics. Slim books instigate revolutions.

The book I hold in my hands has forty-five pages. The cover is black and orange, featuring a ferocious monochrome illustration by the author. 5 x 7 inches. A subtitle appears in the cover's lower right corner, set in an intense, nearly indecipherable font. Two dotted vertical lines run down the cover's center. Tempted, I pick up scissors. Author Mike Corrao's ferocious illustration is the first to fall, followed by the vertical words SURFACE STUDIES. I now have two bookmarks. Yet it feels wrong to stuff them into the maimed little book, like feeding *chicharrón* to a piglet.

What do surface descriptions teach us about literature? Over the course of the twentieth and twenty-first centuries, there have been many attempts at defining a mode of criticism that is so obvious as to be counterintuitive: read closely, but not in the usual places. Various mutations of phenomenological, reader-response, and book-historical modes plumbed the depths of literary perception whilst not disturbing the tranquil waters of structure and form. A superficial, non-exhaustive overview of some of the most cited examples: Louise Rosenblatt (1938) argues that readers matter; Roman Ingarden (1960) observes that meaning peels away in paper-thin layers; Stanley Fish (1967) opines that readers are of many minds; Georges Poulet (1969) wonders if books could talk; Wolfgang Iser (1974) demands that the reader look at themselves in the mirror; Michel de Certeau (1984) charges that the reader is a poacher. These foundational texts, disparate in their motivations, all challenged critics to maintain their identity as *readers*.

More recent examples of reader-centric theory have adopted a more confrontational approach to perception as a mode of criticism. Stephen Best and Sharon Marcus's 2008 article on "surface reading" opens with a provocation: in literary theory, symptom and surface are at war. The former, typified by psychoanalytic and Marxist hermeneutics (most famously in Fredric Jameson's *The Political Unconscious*), basically suggests that in order to reveal meaning, a text must be interrogated, diagnosed, pillaged, or subjected to some other verb borrowed from the military-psychiatric-complex. Surface reading, by contrast, offers a gentler (one could even say nihilistic) approach to criticism, which listens to the text on its own phenomenological terms.

It was this mode of criticism that brought me to read Mike Corrao's *Surface Studies*. Corrao, an interdisciplinary artist, poet, and critic, invites you to judge the book by its cover. But one looks in vain for mention of Fish or Iser or Best/Marcus in its pages. *Surface Studies* is not a scholarly book. The title is therefore deceptive, a Trojan Horse for a footnote-hungry academic: no new subfield is announced, no scholarly literature is reviewed, no footnotes, no bibliography—nothing that gestures, on the surface, to the performative conceit of the title's *Studies*. Rather than build on lit-crit discourse, it performs it. Corrao embodies those unmentioned reader-centric modes of criticism convincingly and inconspicuously, like a method actor deep into character.

Surface Studies looks and feels like the chapbooks it discusses. It unfolds via a series of short "topographical readings" of nine works, cited here in order of appearance: Candice Wuehle's *Death Industrial Complex (2020)*; Evan Isoline's *O! The Scarcity of Gore (2019)*; John Trefry's *Apparitions of the Living (2018)*; Ed Steck's *An Interface for a Fractal Landscape (2019)*; Metahaven's *Digital Tarkovsky (2018)*; M. J. Gette's *Majority Reef (2020)*; Vi Khi Nao's *Sheep Machine (2018)*; Joyelle McSweeney's *Toxicon and Arachne (2020)*; and Olivia Cronk's *Womonster (2020)*. Why bring these nine works together? Some have already been treated in print by Corrao, so *Surface Studies* is partly a compilation of the author's previous reviews. These works could be filed under some wordy sub-sub-subgenre like "post-millennial, pre-pandemic, experimental, indie, underground lit," but even such a monstrosity would not do justice to the more ekphrastic or multimedia works covered here, like *Digital Tarkovsky* and *Majority Reef*.

Instead, what connects these case studies is how they imprint upon Corrao in similar ways. Corrao does not read these works, he moves through them, letting their unique surface topographies guide the way. In his chapter on *Death Industrial Complex*, he calls this "archi-text-ure." Metaphors come and go in *Surface Studies*, some contradictory. While *Majority Reef* is "a living, breathing work of poetry" capable of roots and mutations, a work like *Interface for a Fractal Landscape* is cybernetic, "the raw data of a program and its read-me notes printed and bound." While these modulations seem dizzying, they are also necessary in what Corrao is trying to do. *Surface Studies* dares the reader to look at a page of writing the way a cinematographer peaks through a half-closed fist. To Corrao, the page is a "medium for staging/interfacing/performance." Each text stages its own *mise-en-scène*, its surface tension determining Corrao's analysis down to the keystroke.

Take his chapter on *Apparitions of the Living*, which appears on page eleven with the title "Flesh Objects." Whereas the first ten pages propel the reader with elegant but direct prose (on the very first page he even numbers his concepts, a pedantic move second only to bullet points), "Flesh Objects," with its replacement of punctuation with quasi-stanzaic slashes, shows how deep Corrao will go into his role as surface reader:

> You have before you / a work in the expanded field of literature / John Trefry's *Apparitions of the Living* / a text constructed as if it was an object / with the knowledge that it is an object/ margins grow and shrink / prose condensed into a central column / then stretched across the page / inhaling and exhaling / shifting perspectives / typeset in the digital successor to the Palatino of Robbe-Grillet's *Topology of a Phantom City* / "to which this work is indentured" / a text with physical attributes that cannot be ignored / that lays on the table in front of you / that is read and that knows it is being read //

Can a text "know it is being read?" With that line, Corrao thrusts us back to Poulet and the first reader-responders. *Surface Studies*, maybe despite itself, speaks directly to decades' worth of theory. In fact, it shouts over it, showing and not telling, feeling and not describing. A dangerous little book.

REVIEWS IN BRIEF | Jesi Bender

Magic Can't Save Us: 18 tales of likely failure
Josh Denslow
UNO Press, 2025

In Denslow's short story collection, cryptids and mythological creatures invade everyday life, creating surreal and darkly humorous situations for their human counterparts. What separates this from other 'modern fairytale' books out there is that Denslow has woven these magical beings into everyday situations in a way where each story reads as less like a parable and more like an exploration of the ways in which we use shared stories to understand the strangeness of quotidian life. Particular gems include: "Waves," "Ache," and "Silence."

Disquiet Drive
Hesse K.
Pilot Press, 2024

Disquiet Drive accomplishes what few 'experimental' novels truly do—it challenges form and narrative authority and the reader. In other words, it's original. This book is a scrapbook of a life, an *I*, which is split by circumstance. In the same vein of Eimear McBride's *A Girl is a Half-formed Thing*, K. has created a polyphonic and at times hallucinatory meditation on language and how it is embodied.

Alternative Facts: Stories
Emily Greenberg
Kallisto Gaia Press, 2025

In this collection of short stories, Greenberg embraces our 'post-truth' era where politics has devolved into pop phenomena. The author has an informal, conversational voice that feels like talking with a friend and readers will appreciate her humor and quick pacing. This collection barely predates the current "stupid coup" we're living through but acts as a map to how we got here.

The N-Word of God
Mark Doox
Fantagraphics, 2024

Smart, sad, and horribly beautiful, Mark Doox's literary graphic novel is timely and thought-provoking as it reconceptualizes Abrahamic imagery and teachings to tell the story of what it is to be Black in America. Doox calls his art Byz Dada (Byzantine Dadaism) and seem like they are from gilded illuminated manuscripts, but reimagined with Black representation, including many racial stereotypes. There's Sambo as a saint, Goltzius's Phaeton but with bantu knots, George Washington crossing the Middle Passage, and Our Lady of Ferguson. In one part, a virgin Aunt Jemima is told that she is with child by an angel and she protests, since she "hab bin knowns by a man." But the angel corrects her—"You are mistaken. For he that has been with you and has known you has been legally considered in the past by the Supreme Court of the Land to be only three-fifths a man . . ." Doox reveals horrible aspects of this country in heart break, anger, dark humor, and, yes, even hope as the N-word strung together becomes the cosmic vibration that sustains all of life (. . . NNNNN-NNNNNNN . . .). This is a must-read.

REVIEW | Laney Lenox

You, From Below
Em J Parsley
Split Lip Press
February, 2025

"It's a small memory in the end, as all your memories seem now"—so ruminates the unnamed protagonist (referred to throughout the text and in this review as "you") in Em J Parsley's speculative novella *You, From Below*. The story begins in the quiet aftermath of disaster. An Appalachian holler town has been swallowed by the earth. The town's sole survivor (or, so it seems) carries a mysterious letter in their pocket, knowing intuitively they must deliver it– somewhere, to someone (or something). Along the journey, "you" encounters mythical figures (a possibly immortal woman, a woman left behind by a rapture in her town, a faceless beekeeper), each as alone and lonely as the unnamed protagonist.

That the story begins in the aftermath of the disaster, rather than with the disaster itself, sets a somber and unsettlingly calm tone. The solitary journey of the protagonist reads as a mythological hero's journey through what might be an afterlife; or, perhaps, something that the reader would prefer to think of as an afterlife to avoid the unsettling notion that this world is, in fact, our own.

Reading about a disappeared town in Appalachia immediately called to mind the devastating images of Hurricane Helene from last autumn. In this way, *You, From Below* accomplishes what I enjoy most about speculative fiction and magical realism: using surrealistic imagery and storytelling to expose the strange, unjust, and (in this case) horrific truths of our own world. Having grown up in Louisiana, a place full of wildness, poverty, and particularly vulnerable to the effects of climate change, the uncanny descriptions in *You, From Below* resonated with me deeply. Sometimes you have to tap into the realm of the unreal to accurately portray such places.

As the protagonist recalls people from her now disappeared town (a former partner, a friend from high school, their mother, a gas station employee), I couldn't help but think of the people and livelihoods lost during Hurricane Helene. This is what I love most about *You, From Below* and what I found the most moving– the people's lives that the protagonist recalls throughout the book, memories that they themselves call "small", are elevated to the status of myth– they are worthy of being committed to a kind of immortality through story.

Near the end of the novella, "you" recalls a conversation with their mother in which the mother asks what they would like to do, if they could do anything. "You" responds that they would like to watch the town and its people from a nearby hill. *You, From Below* understands that who and where gets remembered is political and deeply connected to socioeconomic factors. Without giving away the novella's poignant end, I will say that the reader is left with the profound sense that we are inextricably connected to the people in our community and to the physical place itself. These people and these places, especially the ones most vulnerable to natural disasters, climate change, and harsh socioeconomic realities, deserve our attention.

REVIEW | Michael Collins

Solio
Samira Negrouche
Translated by Nancy Naomi Carlson
Seagull Books, May 2024

In the lyric essay "Who is Speaking," Francophone Algerian poet Samira Negrouche imagines greater human consciousness as a poetic lifeworld in which "[s]ilence is a landscape and my ancestors know no borders."[1] Her most recent offering in English, *Solio*, draws us fully *into* this world. Each created in collaboration, one with musicians the other a choreographer, the two books feature dynamic speakers whose movements of music, meditation, and improvisation resonate through Carlson's translations, which are attuned to their interconnections of tone, prosody, form, and perspective. The poems intuitively weave together impressions of other lives: natural, distant, imagined, ancestral—even ours on the impossible side of the page. These figures inhabit worlds woven of the same psychic thread, realizing a *vision* of silence as a cultivated habitat for interiority, the listener woven into a world made of listening.

The opening of "Quay 2|1" invokes this "unsaid elsewhere," its psychic life source both "supported by doubt" and "an invisible thread between my fingers" (5). The speaker channels this imaginal world by entering it:

my arms cross seas
my roots have no anchor
my roots are out of season
don't search for a trace of my voice

---

[1] Samira Negrouche, *The Olive Trees' Jazz*, trans. Marilyn Hacker (Warrensburg, MO: Pleiades Press, 2020), 9.

through you it gathers
through you it unfurls
I even accept the illusion
for us it's a spark
a rousing twilight
a star we invent
a word we hide (6)

An invisible community is formed between speaker and addressees. The paradoxically shared interior "word" both contrasts hollowness and embraces emptiness as potential life:

the white surface isn't the void
nothing isn't the void
what's unsaid about us
isn't the void
I'm not afraid of what's unsaid
nor of the breach concealing time (11)

This space becomes a life source for the speaker,

where I want to think of the nothing that
    opens
where I want to think of the space that
    remains
where I want to believe
that on a snowy trail
a breath lands
and sets down fear. (11)

This incantatory entry into the poem's world accepts "the silence / that isn't trying to fill itself / the silence in disorder" (37). The lyric world both suspends and engages the world of time, conflict, entropy. Through understanding of the worlds' interdependent realities, the speaker is able to hear new inner life emerging:

it's confusion
that makes us two
it's between two
that time
is born
edgeless time
fleeting time
that creates the breach
the lasting breach
there where space
can finally be
touched
between
and between
that touches
there
where
to join.

Something quivers

between
that I don't see
but that I know. (69–70)

Seeing through dualities involved with identity and chronology, the speaker opens the very emptiness through which unforeseen—or previously unseen—life may emerge.

Crucially, these meditative insights may apply concurrently to ontology and creativity. Vibrantly, perhaps reflecting their collaborative and performative genesis, the poems also *live* their central metaphors of form and practice:

I always move
on an uncertain thread
on a certain rupture
and I offer my voice
as I'd offer my cheek
I lengthen my stride
like brushing against
a threshold (13)

The speaker's weaving of this world bypasses logical certitude, following an intuitive process to which "there's nothing disordered / in what comes / how it comes." The weaving equates with a dancer's musical sense: "it dances right / it is announced" (47). This open sense of self as weaving and dancing forms a refrain in "Quay 2| 1":

I'm rooted in movement
time passes through me
beings pass through me
they are me
I am them

These passages evoke a participatory joy in uncertainty: "my steps don't land / they dance / in the elsewhere" (73). In doing so, their genesis offers a rebirth to the world:

I'm rooted in movement
but when I'm rooted
in movement
I unroll
the horizon. (72–3)

This transitory overlapping of selfhoods or self-states—and its correspondence with ongoing worldmaking—deepen awareness of the physical world in "Traces," along with its own instability:

All life is movement, it's one of those
    obvious facts we

nevertheless should remember each day, be
    told each day,
and notice each moment.

The landscape is peaceful, it's only
    conjecture. (84–5)

Being "rooted in movement," in one way, simply means sitting still and really *seeing* how "everything moves, everything is a tangle of pulses, memories, presences, lives, questions." The organic connection between external and interior witnessing in such observation is expressed through a kind of synesthesia: "I listen to silence with my eyes" (85). Such meditations rehearse the intuitive "roots" of the dancing, weaving, and writing so that their creations evoke being per se.

This self-infusing strange loop of consciousness—from meditative observation, to contemplative understanding, to performative creativity in the world—is evoked formally in prose sections using three slashes as breaks:

a finger dips into mercury /// a finger spools
    threads
/// a finger follows you /// a finger measures
    you and
in measuring you, it measures the distance
    /// a finger
scrutinizes you /// a finger asks you the
    question again
/// a finger spins the threads /// a finger
    shakes /// a
finger planes /// a finger wipes the corner of
    the eye ///
a finger extends the invitation /// a finger
    passes
through you. (95)

If the triple slashes are a play on textual commentary's use of a slash to denote a line break, and two slashes a stanza break, this nuance also presents a riddle in form: What is more empty space than a stanza, yet compressed within a line? One answer would be consciousness itself, mirroring the paradox between the poem and the consciousness that formed it, that formed itself in meditative silence.

The "finger" that "Traces" these movements, metaphorically ranging from alchemical to sartorial, alludes to the classical metaphor of weaver as poet. However, exploration of the space between the poles of this metaphor discov-

ers the poem's interdependent creation of self and reader, the poem's own interiority. It has invited us in to show us where we already are.

In "Quay 2|1," consciousness recursively creating itself in its observations and productions presents as a river that "retraces / its flow / even / in the distance" (64), its enduring vitality evoked in the incantatory quickness:

even
in the distance
the river
swelling
in the distance
you arrive
the flows
merge
you arrive (64)

However, these apprehensions of interbeing do not arrive without shadows. "Traces" evokes the restlessness caused by—perhaps also causing—such profound consideration:

I don't sleep at night. when silence falls,
    faces resurface
in my memory, also those I've never seen.

Faces are rooted inside me, all that passed
    by me during
the day and others I haven't seen pass by.

I don't sleep at night, my ears are so
    sensitive, they hear
all the din of the day and, at night, they
    regurgitate the
sounds, they analyze them. (77–9)

At times, the connection between poet and reader allows a symbiotic mode of processing such attendant anxieties, the second person serving as a conduit through which the speaker counsels both the reader and the worried aspect of the self:

You don't want the momentum to worry
    you, you let
the momentum come to you and you think
    that every
momentum is life and death, that every
    momentum is at
first life, is at first a wager you make on life,
    a wager you
win on yourself. (103)

Corollary wisdom regards the abiding of one's self-observations while observing the world:

You can't tell how long it takes for the wave

to calmly
break on you, the halo to move forward, the
    other part
of yourself to depart in the other direction.

The wave passes through you, it seems to
    pass through
you even as it fades into the horizon and you
    move for-
ward, alone, in the other direction.

You don't know how long it takes to pass
    through your
body nor what dwells within you when you
    move for-
ward, alone, in the other direction.

Now that you're walking alone again, you
    become the
wave, you become the deep breath of the
    wave. (106–7)

Deep identity is both inherently universal and endlessly mutable. The world flows over and through psyche as psyche moves through the world. The constructed identities of which we convince ourselves, though necessary to function in the social world, are secondary realities in the meditator's witness of being itself, "rooted in the movement"—as well as the poet's weaving and singing it back to itself.

From the perspective of the ego, such experiences of interbeing imply limitation even as they invite one to potential transformation: "If I speak to you, I speak through what we lack. This lack is our chance, the only true excuse for venturing out on the road" (111). With diligent presence, however, we may even become ancestors ourselves: "I came from an earlier time / to remind you of the promise of dawn" (112). Here, again, we return to the paradoxes between psy-

chological and chronological time that help to structure these poems. In places, they also show how the speaker's meditative identity, studied in emulation of the ancestors, and her temporal activity as a poet, weave together:

I came from that time that amasses horizons
and sifts through them
one by one, with care
giving each its measure. (112)

The senses of proportion in composition of crafted work and fluid perception bear an uncanny resemblance to one another—in ways that freely transfer to the reader's fostering of their own practices. These poems, indeed, have moved far from the questions with which we opened, their process itself a fluid and resilient rooting in movement between individual, image, nature, other—between being and interbeing. It is only fitting to conclude with a passage that reads as their self-description:

I'm not afraid of emptiness
emptiness isn't nothing
emptiness is along the thread
the uncertain thread
the invisible thread
on which I suspend existence
on which existence suspends me
wherever it happens
wherever it clings (14)

CHRISTOPHER BOUCHER

EXACT NG B RD

I'd just started writing my story for *Exacting Clam 17* when I heard this chirping sound in the corner of the page, looked up into the title, and spotted a small red bird perched on the numbers—one foot on the 8 and the other on the 9.

"Oh," I said. "Hello there."

The bird gazed over the sentences I'd just written. Then it darted to the first one, stole the "I" from it, and flew back to the top of the page.

"Hey!" I said. "That's my I!"

The bird dropped the I on the 89, swooped back down to fetch the i in chirping, and returned to its perch. Then it swallowed the lowercase letter—despite my hollering—took the uppercase letter in its beak, and flew off.

I looked down at the sentence, which now read "... when heard this ch rping sound in the corner of the page . . ." I had some extra letters on hand, luckily, so I fixed the sentence—swearing to myself the whole time—and continued on with my work.

The next morning, though, I came back to the story and found it decimated. Not only were the replacement Is gone, but others had been removed too. "Then t darted over to the f rst one, stole the " " from t . . . ," read the third paragraph now. I walked down to the sixth paragraph and saw, " had some extra letters on hand, luck ly, so f xed the sentence . . ." The story was in shambles—it didn't even make any sense now!

Fuming, I stormed over to some other selections. Sure enough, the bird had nicked some of their Is as well. "Marvin Cohen on Hearing" now contained phrases like "Here am," and "The nstruments for th s are talk ng, see ng . . ." Hilbert's poem "Nineteen Locks" was hit too—"Your shapes and l nes, the s gns that greet your s ght."—as well as Stannard's essay: "Yet as a young Engl shman now based n Genoa wanted to f nd an tal an poet whose wr t ng resonated . . ."

The editors called a meeting in Clam Tower that afternoon to discuss the "exact ng b rd problem." Sal Vincent, an experienced hunter, said she'd be happy to take care of it. "Take care of it how?" said Helen Marsh.

"You know how," Sal said, making her hand into the shape of a pistol.

"Shoot a helpless little bird?" Marsh said.

"This helpless little bird's costing us a lot of money," said Cordelia Twice. "These   letters aren't free!"

"What does it want with them, anyway?" asked Sigh Becker from the corner of the room.

"I think it eats them," I said.

Twice turned to face me. "*Eats* them?"

"I saw it eat a lowercase one," I said.

"Yuck," said Marsh.

"Anyway, there must be a more humane option," Sigh said. "Is there such a thing as literary animal control?"

"Animal control my ass," said Sal. "If I see that bird I'm taking it out."

The b rd—or b rds?—struck tw ce more that week. The first t me t picked at Shya Scanlon's "An American Story" (" t couldn't have been nc dental that both these authors were aston sh ngly accompl shed . . ."). But the b rd also came back to my story, pull ng every s ngle out of th s paragraph. Why was t p ck ng on me? Could t have known was wr t ng a story about t? D d b rds *read*?

As long as our feathered foe was at large, Marsh ordered us to use as few s as we could. "Less for the foul fowl to steal," she'd told us. The staff worked to comply—all of us except for Sal, who started walking through the journal with a r fle on her back.

That Thursday afternoon, I was working on the end of the story when I heard that familiar chirping again. I followed the sound off the page and out to the end of the book. There, in the dark corner where the page met the back cover, was a whole bundle of uppercase Is, all packed tightly in horizontal rows.

Suddenly Sal appeared next to me, her rifle in her arms. "I heard the chirping," she said. "What is that friggin' thing?"

Just then a bird's head appeared out of the Is.

"Holy shit it's a nest," she whispered.

"Come on, Sal," I said. "You can't kill a bird in its nest."

"Wanna bet?" she said, raising her rifle. "Goodbye you I-stealing—"

But just then a second head—the head of a tiny baby bird—appeared in the nest. And then another tiny bird's face, and then another. The tiny birds were chirping and squawking—they were hungry.

"Don't you dare, Sal," I said.

Sal sighed and lowered the gun. Then we both watched as the exact ng b rd fetched a lowercase i—maybe even one of mine—and dropped it into the newborn bird's open beak.

Contributors

Roberta Allen, a Tennessee Williams Fellow in Fiction and a Yaddo Fellow, has nine published books, including three collections of very short and short fiction, a novel, a novella in flash fictions and a memoir. Her latest collection is *The Princess of Herself*. Over 200 stories have appeared in journals, including *Conjunctions* and *Epoch*, *New World Writing* and the *Evergreen Review*.

Jesi Bender is an artist from Upstate New York. She is the author of the novels *Child of Light* (forthcoming) and *The Book of the Last Word* (Whiskey Tit), the play *Kinderkrankenhaus* (Sagging Meniscus), and the chapbook *Dangerous Women* (dancing girl press). Her shorter work can be found in *FENCE, Vol. 1 Brooklyn*, *Sleepingfish*, and others.

Jacek Blaszkiewicz is an assistant professor of music history at Wayne State University in Detroit, Michigan. His first book, *Fanfare for a City: Music and the Urban Imagination in Haussmann's Paris*, was published in 2024 by the University of California Press.

P.J. Blumenthal, an American writer in Munich, Germany, writes in both German and English. He is the author of *Winston Hewlett's Impotence* (Sagging Meniscus, 2024), a non-fiction book on feral man, *Kaspar Hausers Geschwister* (Kaspar Hauser's Siblings), and a German-language blog, "Der Sprachbloggeur."

Christopher Boucher is the author of the novels *How to Keep Your Volkswagen Alive* (Melville House, 201), *Golden Delicious* (MH, 2016), and *Big Giant Floating Head* (MH, 2019). He teaches writing and literature at Boston College and is Managing Editor of *Post Road Magazine*.

Ian Boulton is a UK-based writer. He has been a regular contributor to several magazines, both online and in print, including *The Rusty Nail, Notes From The Underground, Literary Juice, Sentinel Literary Quarterly* and others. His stories have been appearing in *Exacting Clam* since 2022. "Triptych-on-Sea", which appeared in the Autumn 2024 edition, was nominated for The Pushcart Prize.

Graham Clifford is an award-winning British poet published by *Seren, Against the Grain* and *BLER*. Born in Portsmouth, he now lives in London with his partner and two daughters. Graham earns his money as a Head teacher in Tower Hamlets.

Marvin Cohen (1931–2025) was the author of many novels, plays, and collections of essays, stories, and poems. He lived on the Lower East Side of Manhattan.

Michael Collins' poems and book reviews have received Pushcart Prize nominations and appeared in more than 70 journals and magazines. He is the author of the chapbooks *How to Sing when People Cut off your Head and Leave it Floating in the Water* and *Harbor Mandala* and the full-length collections *Psalmandala* and *Appearances*, named one of the best indie poetry collections of 2017 by Kirkus Reviews. He teaches creative and expository writing at New York University and has taught at The Hudson Valley Writer's Center, The Bowery Poetry Club, and several community outreach and children's centers in Westchester. He is the Poet Laureate of Mamaroneck, NY.

Kevin Davey is the author of *English Imaginaries*, an account of the transformation of Englishness in the twentieth century (2000). As a director of The Innovatory he mentored a large number of creative businesses in London before writing a trilogy of experimental fictions: *Playing Possum* (2017), *Radio Joan* (2020) and *Toothpull of St Dunstan* (2025), all published by Aaaargh! Press. These texts engage with turning points in English history, using peripheral spaces as a constraint, and twentieth century modernism—particularly Eliot, Pound, and Khlebnikov—as a compass.

W.J. Davies' essays and reviews can be found in *Literary Review, Review 31, Slightly Foxed* and elsewhere. His story 'Pest Problem' is included in Brilliant Flash Fiction's 2024 anthology, and he has been shortlisted for a Cranked Anvil fiction prize. He lives in South East England.

Gina DeMartino, writer and artist, recently graduated with her BA in Visual Arts at Montclair State University. Through her acrylic paper collages, she curates colorful adventures of queer relationships and self portraits exploring both uncertainty and acceptance of the self.

Rose Facchini is a Lecturer in Italian at Tufts University and the Editor and Italian Translator Editor for the *International Poetry Review*. Her translations have either appeared or are forthcoming in *Asymptote*'s Translation Tuesdays, *West Branch, ergot., Heimat Review, Fictive Dream, Exacting Clam, Wyldblood, 365tomorrows, Intrinsick*, and *International Poetry Review*, and she has read her translation of Diego Lama's flash fiction story "Freedom" ["Libertà"] on Translators Aloud.

Alban Fischer is the author of the poetry collection *Fake Moon* and founding editor of Trnsfr Books. He lives in Michigan, where he makes his living as a book designer.

M.J. Gilbert is the author of *The Riddle of Firelight, A Most Curious Winter's Tale* and, more recently, *The Rival Poet*, an experimental collection of poetry. He holds a PhD in Literature from Stony Brook University, where he studied the influence of music on the poetry of British Romanticism.

Jake Goldsmith is a writer with cystic fibrosis and the founder of The Barbellion Prize, a book prize for ill and disabled authors. He is the author of *Neither Weak Nor Obtuse* (SM, 2022) and *In Hospital Environments: Essays on Illness and Philosophy* (SM, 2024).

Jeffrey Hecker is author of *Rumble Seat* (San Francisco Bay Press, 2011) & chapbooks *Hornbook* (Horse Less Press, 2012), *Instructions for the Orgy* (Sunnyoutside Press, 2013) & *Ark Aft* (The Magnificent Field, 2020). Recent work appears in *South Dakota Review* and *Bennington Review*. A fourth-generation Kepanī via Hawaii, he teaches at The Muse Writers Center & reads for *Quarterly West*.

John Patrick Higgins is a writer and director. He is the author of *Teeth* (SM, 2024), *Fine* (SM, 2024), and *Spine* (SM, 2025). He lives in Belfast, where it rains.

Ernest Hilbert is the author of the poetry collections *Sixty Sonnets, All of You on the Good Earth, Caligulan*—selected as winner of the 2017 Poets' Prize—and *Last One Out*. His fifth book, *Storm Swimmer*, was selected by Rowan Ricardo Phillips as the winner of the 2022 Vassar Miller Prize and appeared in 2023. He lives in Philadelphia.

John Oliver Hodges lives in New Jersey. His writing has appeared in numerous print and online journals, including *Black Scat Review, The Decadent Review, Thin Air Magazine* and *New World Writing*. His collection of short stories, *The Love Box*, won the Tartt First Fiction Award, and includes photos. He has a novel out called *Quizzleboon* and two memoirs forthcoming: *Our Dad the Commie* (Frayed Edge Press) and *Kill the Punks* (Panhandle Punk), which recalls his time in Hated Youth, an American Hardcore band from Florida during the 1980s. John teaches writing at the Gotham Writers' Workshop.

Charles Holdefer's latest book is *Ivan the Terrible Goes on a Family Picnic* (SM, 2024).

Carl Landauer taught history at Yale, Stanford, and McGill. He has written broadly on intellectual and cultural history and the history of law. He has published articles and book reviews with *Salmagundi, Renaissance Quarterly, Yale Journal of Law & the Humanities, German Studies Review, Confrontations, Beat Scene, American Scholar*, the *San Francisco Chronicle, Newsday*, and *Poetry Flash*.

Laney Lenox is an anthropologist, researcher, and writer from Louisiana living in Berlin, Germany with her husband. She has an interdisciplinary PHD in anarchist political theory and memory studies. Writing featured in *Salvation South, Ghost City Review, A Thin Slice of Anxiety* and elsewhere.

Roy Lisker (1938–2019) was a writer, artist, mathematician, journalist and political activist. He was the author of a vast amount of literature in every imaginable form, which he largely self-distributed to friends and subscribers to his newsletter, *Ferment*. His conventionally published work includes *In Memoriam Einstein* (SM, 2016) and *Lincoln Center in July* (SM, 2016).

Kurt Luchs is the author of *Tributaries* (SM, 2025), *Death Row Row Row Your Boat* (SM, 2024), *Falling in the Direction of Up* (SM, 2021), *One of These Things Is Not Like the Other* (Finishing Line Press, 2019), and *It's Funny Until Someone Loses an Eye (Then It's Really Funny)* (SM, 2017). He lives in Michigan.

Irene Moccia was the recipient of the Carlo Levi Poetry Prize in 2019. She has performed her poetry, which focuses on female identity, body consciousness, and the magic of the mundane, in various festivals throughout Italy. She holds a Law Degree and is currently working as Human Resources legal counsel in an insurance company. Her project Ritenzione lirica aims to disseminate poetry on social media.

Dan Morey is a freelance writer based in Pennsylvania. His creative work has appeared in *Hobart, Great Lakes Review, McSweeney's Quarterly, Johnny America* and elsewhere.

REYoung was born in Pittsburgh, Pennsylvania, and currently resides in a limestone cave deep beneath the city of Austin, Texas. He is the author of five novels: *Unbabbling* (Dalkey Archive Press, 1996), *Margarito and the Snowman* (Dalkey Archive Press, 2016), *Inflation* (TageTage Press, 2019), *The Ironsmith* (TageTage Press, 2020) and *Zol* (TageTage Press, 2020).

David Rose, born 1949, resident in Britain, is now retired after a working life in the Post Office. His short stories are published widely in the UK and US, including in *The Penguin Book of the Contemporary Short Story* (ed. Philip Hensher, 2018) and partly collected in *Posthumous Stories* (Salt, 2013). He is the author of two novels: *Vault* (Salt, 2011) and *Meridian* (Unthank Books, 2015).

Christopher Carter Sanderson is the translator/adaptor of *The Support Verses* and author of the novel *The Too-Brief Chronicle of Judah Lowe*. His poetry can be found in literary magazines and anthologies, and he contributes to notable trade publications. He is an ASCAP composer, Dramatists Guild playwright, SDC theatrical director, visual artist with Gather Gallery, and founded Gorilla Rep in NYC.

Shya Scanlon is the author of the novel *The Guild of Saint Cooper*, and the poetry collection *In This Alone Impulse*. His stories and nonfiction have been published widely but sporadically. He lives in upstate New York with his wife and their dog.

Mike Silverton is the author of *Anvil on a Shoestring* (SM, 2022), *Trios* (SM, 2023), and *Yoga for Pickpockets* (SM, 2024).

RW Spryszak's work has appeared in the alternative press since the late 1980's. His latest short novel is *Drainman* (Alien Buddha Press, July 2024).

Lucian Staiano-Daniels is a historian of violent conflict who was educated at St. John's College, NYU, and UCLA.

Julian Stannard currently teaches English Literature and Creative Writing at the University of Winchester. He taught for many years at the University of Genoa. He has written about Genoa and Liguria in his poetry. *Sottoripa: Genoese Poems*—a bilingual project—was published in 2018 by Canneto. In 2024 he was awarded the Lerici Shelley Prize for his contribution to Anglo-Ligurian literature. His *New And Selected Poems* (Salt, 2025) contains many of his Italian poems. A satirical novel—*The University of Bliss*—was published by Sagging Meniscus Press in 2024.

Joe Taylor is the author of numerous novels and collections of short fiction. He has directed Livingston Press at the University of West Alabama since 1990, and, appropriately for a publisher of thoughtful, innovative fiction, he and his wife Tricia house over a dozen stray dogs, who mostly do not savage him.

Stefano De Vecchi works in hospice. He likes taking strolls, playing soccer, and going to the library to write down anything that inspires him.

Bradley David Waters is a writer of poetry, fiction, hybrid, and essays. His writing and image-work appears in *Terrain.org, Denver Quarterly, HAD, The Los Angeles Review* and numerous other publications and anthologies. He is also the blended-genre senior editor at *jmww* journal. Bradley and his husband split their time between Southern and Northern California, wrangling chickens and fussing over fruit trees.

www.ingramcontent.com/pod-product-compliance
Lightning Source LLC
Chambersburg PA
CBHW081522050726
47503CB00018B/2950